Unleash Your Inner Tyrant!

Proven Strategies to Help ***You*** Become a Terrible Boss

Jeff Havens

Unleash Your Inner Tyrant!

Printed in the United States of America.

ISBN-13: 978-0-9843022-3-9
ISBN-10: 0-9843022-3-9

Published by Big Pow! Books
207 W. Jefferson St., #503
Bloomington, IL 61704
www.gobigpow.com

Cover design by Adam Havens

Dedication

To all the overbearing, uncooperative, manipulative, and otherwise horrible bosses, managers, and other employees who suck the joy out of work every day, without whom this book could not have been written.

Unleash Your Inner Tyrant!

Proven Strategies to Help *You*

Become a Terrible Boss

Section Three:
OUTSOURCE BLAME

Section Four:
RESIST CHANGE

Section Five:
THE TRUTH ABOUT LEADERSHIP

Author's Note

Just to be perfectly clear, this is not going to be your typical leadership book. I've read my fair share of books about leadership, and here's a little secret: *they're all exactly the same.* They each have different stories and anecdotes, different statistics and references, but every one of them tells you what you *should* be doing. As far as I can tell, there hasn't been a single leadership book written about what *not* to do, that focuses on *worst* practices, the things we're all occasionally guilty of and should strive to avoid. There isn't a single leadership book that strives to teach through negative example, to 'encourage' you to engage in all the behaviors you know you shouldn't engage in. And since such an approach has the potential to be *way* more entertaining than a more straightforward take on leadership, I decided to write it myself.

So here it is, the best leadership book in the history of ever. I'm fairly certain you'll get a decent amount of laughs out of this book. But be warned. If you're not careful, you might accidentally learn something.

Hope you enjoy.

Jeff Havens

Why You Need This Book

Welcome, and congratulations on either purchasing, stealing, or receiving from a sycophantic colleague your very own copy of *Unleash Your Inner Tyrant!* By choosing to open this book, you have made quite possibly the most important decision of your life. You've chosen to reject the conventional wisdom about leadership, that insufferable claptrap that has made our business world such a drab and boring place. You've seen your high-powered colleagues with their winning smiles and legions of adoring followers, their pictures featured in *Fortune* and *Fast Times* alongside taglines like "100 Best Managers" and "Best Places to Work." You've seen these people with their staid ties and trite aphorisms, and you've thought to yourself as you've listened to yet another employee leave your office in tears, *That's not going to happen to me.*

So again, congratulations on finding this book.

Unleash Your Inner Tyrant! is going to open up a beautiful new world for you. Most people would call it a 180 degree departure from the business books you're familiar with, but I like to think of it as a *540* degree departure, an approach so revolutionary and amazing that it will not surprise me if I am immediately appointed to key positions in either the Russian, North Korean, or Iranian governments upon this book's publication.

Now I know you've read other books on leadership. They're impossible to avoid; in fact, in 2004 there were 6,707 titles on leadership registered at the Library of Congress. I've seen you rifling idly through the leadership book you were given by the keynote speaker at that last conference you attended, a crappy prize for having suffered through his crappy speech – one more thing for you to lug home, one more 'sale' that he or she can pretend to have made. I've seen you skimming the business section at the airport bookstore, looking for the perfect book to help you sleep through your five-hour flight to Seattle. I've seen you at your desk, pretending to read the latest leadership book your boss called a real game-changer, all the while wondering how anybody who uses phrases like 'game-changer' could possibly be higher up in the company than you. I've seen you read leadership book after leadership book in order to keep up the pretense that you're deeply interested in your own continual improvement, and I know that playing this ridiculous charade has gradually worn you down.

Even worse, I know you've accidentally absorbed some of the material in all of these books, seminars, conferences, précis, and executive summaries. And some of the garbage those so-called 'experts' on leadership come up with…well, quite frankly it boggles the mind.

Stupid Ideas You've Heard in the Past – And Are Likely to Hear Again

- Servant Leadership
- Partnership

- Treating Your Employees Like Equals
- Listening to Other People's Ideas
- Taking Responsibility for Your Failures
- Creating Win/Win Situations
- Embracing Change
- Facing Reality
- Trusting Your Employees
- Avoiding Micromanagement at All Costs

Are you kidding me? Seriously, who wants to do these things? Not me. The very idea of engaging in productive and meaningful teamwork turns my stomach. Listening to other people's thoughts has never failed to make my blood pressure rise, and don't even get me started on the dangers of *'win-win'* outcomes. And I'm willing to bet that you don't like any of those ideas either, which is why I've written this book. In fact, if you're honest with yourself, you'll admit that you've been searching for this book your entire professional life. You've read books with titles like *The 18 Secrets of People Better than You* and *The 48 Cylinders of Awesomeness*, searching in vain for new and exciting ways to oppress and demoralize those unfortunate enough to fall into your orbit.

Until now.

Unleash Your Inner Tyrant! follows the practices of some of the world's most domineering and autocratic leaders and will help you learn the secrets of their respective tyrannies. We're going to show you the time-tested practices of such despotic visionaries as Henry Ford, Stuart Parnell, Joseph Stalin, Jeffrey Skilling, Harry Cohn, Alan Schwartz, Bernard Ebbers, Donald Trump, Harold Geneen, and so many others, leaders whose subordinates hoped and prayed every day for their forced retirement or premature death – the kind of 'leaders' you've always wanted to emulate. I'm going to give you the tools necessary to drain all the joy out of those around you, to ensure that the healthy, vibrant corporate culture you've inherited is not one you'll have to tolerate for very much longer.

According to research conducted by Harvard University, 85% of a leader's performance depends on personal character.

And that's not all. Because I realize you might despair of ever becoming as effective a tyrant as somebody like Al Dunlap, who in 2000 was voted by Conde Nast Porfolio.com the 6th worst CEO of all time.[1] So I'll also regale you with real-life stories of everyday tyrannies from everyday people just like yourselves, stories collected both from personal experience and from some of the thousands of businessmen and women I've had the opportunity to meet over the last several years. By the end of this book, you will have learned several things:

1) That becoming a tyrant is not a skill reserved for only the strongest or most ambitious, but rather is something available to each and every one of us

[1] Unfortunately for Al, his ranking has probably fallen a few spots since then, as there have been some unbelievably successful tyrants in the past 10 years.

2) That the tools you need in order to begin, perfect, and sustain your tyranny are already available to you and waiting to be exploited
3) That in some cases you've been engaging in various tyrannical behaviors for quite some time now, and kudos to you for doing so!
4) That *Unleash Your Inner Tyrant!* is the best and most important book in the history of ever, one you will undoubtedly buy for all of your friends and whose personal copy you will eventually bequeath to your favorite child

In short, I'm going to provide you with a well-tested, step-by-step process to establish your own tyrannical working environment. Most business books give you advice, whatever that word means. *Unleash Your Inner Tyrant!*, on the other hand, gives you *permission* to do the kinds of things you've wanted to do all along.

So, would you like your subordinates to scamper down alternate hallways when they see you coming? Would you like your employees to sing "Happy Birthday" to you in the same hateful, lifeless way that Initech's workers sang to Bill Lundberg? Then look no further, my aspiring megalomaniac. *Unleash Your Inner Tyrant!* is the only book you'll ever need to read again.[2]

---

[2] We've actually just illustrated one of the easiest ways to begin your fledgling tyranny: pretending that others have answered rhetorical questions. It's a great way to create the illusion that others actually agree with you, and it's also extremely annoying. A tip of the hat to the hundreds and hundreds of business speakers who have perfected this technique. Without their near-constant use of it, I might have accidentally overlooked its potential.

What Your Employees Want

Before we can begin establishing your tyranny, it will help to have a consistent idea of what exactly your employees want and need in order to be successful. There have been countless studies and surveys designed to discover the secrets of a happy and productive workforce, which of course means it's virtually impossible to compile a fully accurate list. However, my research has led me to the following, which we will be using for the purposes of this book. These items are not necessarily in order of importance, nor do they need to be, as an effective tyrant is always working to be equally tyrannical in every possible way.

Requirements of Happy, Successful, Productive, Loyal Employees

- They have a salary and benefits package that allows them to provide for all their immediate needs
- They know what is expected of them at work
- They have easy access to necessary materials
- They receive regular praise and recognition for good work
- They have a healthy professional and personal relationship with their immediate superior
- They agree with the main purpose of the company they work for and believe their work is

making the world better for someone in some way

- They have close relationships with their coworkers
- They have the opportunity to learn, grow, and move up in the company
- They have superiors who actively encourage and provide opportunities for their professional development
- They have occasional conversations with their immediate superiors about advancement, career goals, job satisfaction, and other psychological intangibles
- They feel secure in their job and believe their company will make every effort to save their job should things become difficult
- They believe their opinion and expertise is taken into consideration by their immediate supervisors on issues of problem-solving, professional development, etc.

None of this should be surprising, and all of it should sound like things you've read before. But as I've already mentioned, it helps to have a good working model. You should now know what your employees are looking for.

And now it's time to start denying them everything they want.

The Tetrarchy of Tyranny

So let's get right to it, the keys to an effective tyranny. Like all good business authors, I too have devised a pseudo-elaborate system of organizing and sharing my brilliance.

And here it is. Almost everything I'm going to discuss in this book can be placed into one of four major courses of action, a program of oppression that I like to call The Tetrarchy of Tyranny.

In the first section – *Create an Environment of Fear, Self-Interest, and Mistrust* – we'll set the appropriate tone. Before you can have a fully operational tyranny, you'll first need to create an environment in which your tyrannical qualities can thrive. Because you've probably been brainwashed by all those other business books you've been pressured into reading, I've designed this section as a gentle introduction, a way for you to ease yourself into your tyranny in much the same way you might ease yourself into a steaming hot tub after a long day of brutalizing those who work for you.

It should go without saying that the second section – *Trample Your Underlings…Then Trample Them Again!* – is my personal favorite. This is where you'll learn the myriad techniques to systematically cajole, threaten, pummel, abuse, disrespect, ignore, infuriate, condemn, and otherwise torment the people who work for you. This section serves an important dual purpose as well. For while it's designed as a learning tool and is in fact a very effective one, it's also the most purely enjoyable piece of everything we'll be discussing. Trampling your underlings is fun, people! So get ready to enjoy this section the way that you enjoy playing whack-a-mole at your local arcade. Because if you're not giddy with glee at all the ideas you'll come across in *Trample Your Underlings...*, then you are probably missing a decent portion of your brain.

In *Outsource Blame* we'll discuss the various ways that a good tyrant handles the persistent issue of responsibility. One caveat here - the section title, while amazing and awesome, is a bit of a misnomer. Because while you will certainly learn how to blame others for your own failures, this section will also teach you how to take credit for other people's successes as well. This is one of the easiest sections in the entire book, as it's a skill you have probably been practicing since you were teething. Chances are you're already a master at this - and if you think you aren't, then you definitely are.

In *Resist Change,* I'll show you how to stand firm against any ideas, policies, and practices that you did not think up yourself. This, of course, is a favorite tactic of some of the successfully repressive dictatorships the world has ever seen. Now, most self-professed 'leadership experts' argue that resistance to the natural evolution of business is nothing short of suicidal. But I contend that it is instead a valiant stand against the subtle forces that might threaten your hegemony. This section also includes some extremely important advice about what to do if you should ever find power slipping from your grasp (hint: the answer does not involve going down without a fight!)

There's another section as well - *The Truth About Leadership* - which doesn't technically fit into The Tetrarchy of Tyranny but which I felt was necessary for this book, and which is perhaps the most diabolical section of them all. Why? Because of all five sections, it alone contains the secrets of *good* leadership, all the best ideas and practices that have been culled from years of personal experience, study, and management research.

Why on Earth would I include such an absurd section in a book about unleashing your inner tyrant? Because eventually, the process of unleashing your inner tyrant will most likely cost you your job. Either your superiors will grow weary of the constant complaints about your leadership style and will reluctantly offer you a meager severance package so that you can 'explore new opportunities,' or the people beneath you will rise up against their oppressor and stage a bloodless coup that will end with you in the street and your retractable keycard hanging from the ramparts of your former office kingdom. And when that inevitable day of reckoning comes, you'll need to know how to go about getting another job *so you can begin your tyranny anew.* As long as you know how to fool people into thinking that you actually care about their well-being, you should be able to establish a new tyranny anytime, anywhere.

So what are you waiting for? Are you ready to leave a swath of destruction in your wake that will take your company years to recover from? Are you ready to start acquiring nicknames like "Career Killer," "Schizophrenic Windbag," "Bosshole," and all the others that you've dreamed about since you were a child? Are you ready for joy to wither at your approach, for flowers to die when you look at them, for your subordinates to willfully pour scalding coffee onto themselves so they can take a medical leave of absence and escape your everpresent wrath for a few glorious hospital-bound days? Are you ready to finally give in to your heart's whisperings and unleash your inner tyrant?

The path to your greatness is in front of you. All you have to do is turn the page.

Create an Environment of Fear, Self-Interest, and Mistrust

Establish Positional Dominance!

"Power corrupts. Absolute power is kind of neat."
John Lehman

"I can no longer obey. I have tasted command, and I cannot give it up."
Napoleon Bonaparte

Tyranny. Such a beautiful word, isn't it? It just rolls off the tongue, simple and sonorous, like 'leather' or 'sluices.' I'm sure you've whispered it to yourself as you've sat at your desk, trying to figure out how you could inspire nothing but contempt and loathing in everyone forced to work for you. Perhaps you've made a few tentative attempts at establishing your own tyranny - yelling at subordinates for minor mistakes, shouting down your employees' ideas before they had a chance to finish talking, ignoring everyone with a less expensive car than you.

But until now your efforts have been scattered and disorganized, at times even amateurish. They've lacked cohesion. They've lacked *a system*. Which of course is what this book is all about, providing you with the tools you need to unleash your inner tyrant to greatest effect.

Now it should be obvious that before you can become a successful tyrant, you first need to create an environment in which your tyrannical qualities can thrive. Fortunately for the purposes of this book, the environment in question is the same no matter where you work. Whether you work in a factory, office building, airplane hangar, converted shed, retail store, family farm, nightclub, day spa, high rise, low rise, medium rise, your parent's garage, or a secret underground government facility, the same trinity predominates:

Fear - The more people fear and despise you (and each other, if you're any good at this), the more effective your tyranny will be.

Self-Interest - Focus on your own goals to the exclusion of everyone else's. It's simple, effective, and a lot of fun!

Mistrust - A good tyrant[1] never overlooks the opportunity to sow discord and suspicion into the ranks of his or her subordinates. After all, without mistrust, there can be no real oppression. Not to mention that trust breeds

[1] Do yourself the favor of ignoring the obvious oxymoron inherent in 'good tyrant.' In fact, you should probably ignore every contradiction and otherwise nonsensical piece of information you receive in this book. Good tyrants – yes, I said that on purpose – good tyrants are neither consistent nor rational, facts which we will discuss in greater detail in subsequent chapters.

comfort, and it's hard to make people hate you when they feel comfortable.

There is a slim chance that such an environment already exists in your workplace; after all, plenty of professional environments already possess the dreary and soul-crushing qualities you should be striving for. And if yours already fits the bill, then feel free to exploit what you've been given.

If not, however, and instead your workplace is healthy and vibrant, you'll need to begin the process of dismantling it. I don't want to lie to you – creating this culture can be a lot of work. However, I promise it will repay itself in the scarcely-veiled animosity you'll be able to see in the faces of everyone unfortunate enough to work for you.

The first step in creating an environment of fear, self-interest, and mistrust is to establish positional dominance – or, as I like to call it, ***Laying the Smack Down!*** The people who work for you need to know who the boss is. And the boss, in case it's not obvious, is *you*.

According to a 2007 study, 40% of all employees say they work for bad bosses.

Profiles in Tyranny: Harry Cohn

Periodically throughout this book we will be examining the lives and careers of various brutish, conniving, immoral, megalomaniacal, and otherwise tyrannical leaders. It is the intention of each *Profile in Tyranny* to provide you with at least one concrete example of a specific tyrannical leadership

technique, so that you can better hone your abilities through emulation. For those of you who enjoy history, many of these *Profiles in Tyranny* will be both a nostalgic remembrance of things past and a collection of stories that should make you wonder how civilized humanity ever managed to survive as long as it has.

And for those of you who don't enjoy history, read these anyway.

Our first *Profile in Tyranny* is Harry Cohn, founder and first president of Columbia Pictures. It's often said that the measure of a man can be determined by what those closest to him say about him when he's not around. Well if that's true, then Cohn is an excellent place for us to begin. One subordinate described him as – and I quote – "as absolute a monarch as Hollywood ever knew;" another affectionately called him "White Fang." Orson Welles, the famed filmmaker and UFO eyewitness, described Cohn as a "monster" who tended to snarl rather than speak. And for the icing on Cohn's tyrannical cake, it is said that of the approximately 1,300 people who attended his funeral in 1958, the vast majority were there to assure themselves that he was actually dead.[2] You can only hope to be so lucky.

Cohn employed several techniques to ensure that everyone who worked for him knew exactly who was boss. He kept an autographed portrait of Benito Mussolini on his desk at all times, a man Cohn apparently admired after having met him in 1933. He also developed a habit of holding a riding

[2] Upon hearing of his death, Red Skelton was quoted thusly: "It proves what Harry always said: give the public what they want, and they'll come out for it."

whip in one hand while talking to his employees, which he would systematically smack into the other hand to emphasize particularly unfriendly points. I think it goes without saying that Cohn frothed at the mouth whenever he shouted his displeasure at those beneath him. And if there's any lesson you should take away from him, let it be this: never overlook the power of a few well-placed droplets of rage-generated spittle.

But that's not all. Cohn also installed hidden microphones on all the sets and in all the offices at Columbia. Big Brother was indeed watching, and Cohn became famous for periodically shouting at his actors over the set loudspeakers if he heard them saying something he disapproved of. In all ways, Cohn made himself the king of his fiefdom, and he let his subjects know that as often as he possibly could.

So there you have it, people. The more rigidly you enforce your management hierarchy, the more despotic you will appear to those beneath you. And that's perfectly fine. Why? Because they *are* beneath you. And you should never let them forget it.

Cohn, as you can tell, never let his employees forget that he was in command, and it's one of the many reasons that so many people were so happy to hear that he had died.

However, many of his approaches to establishing positional dominance are either outdated or impractical. For example, you might have trouble getting Mussolini to sign a picture of himself so that you can display it prominently on your steel-and-glass desk. And seriously, a riding whip? Unless your cousin is a jockey, chances are you don't have one of those lying around. Not to mention that placing surveillance equipment in all of your employees' wastebaskets is, in many cases, cost-prohibitive. Trust me – I've looked into it.

But don't despair. There are still several simple things you can do to demonstrate your invariable superiority over those beneath you. Each of these approaches is market-tested, and hopefully you're already doing at least one of them. Let's find out!

Chairman Jeff's Simple Steps to a More Domineering You!

- *Corner offices!* Nothing like having *two* walls of windows to remind your subordinates that they have no windows at all.
- *Doors!* Who'd have thought that a flat slab of particle board could make such a big difference?
- ***Luxury office furniture!*** Does your chair swivel? Mine does.
- ***Engraved, embossed, or otherwise permanent nameplates!*** Your employees probably have inexpensive nameplates – pieces of formica taped to their carpeted cubicle walls, or maybe a bi-fold formica tent that sits on their desks. The point is, theirs is definitely made out of formica, which is cheap and easy to replace, much like the employee whose name is stenciled in it. The fact that your nameplate is etched on your glass door

or chiseled into the floor by the elevator will send an important message. You are here to stay. They…not so much.

- ***Subtle differentiation of your business card and letterhead stationery!*** The fact that nobody but you would even notice such a thing is all the more reason to do it.

- ***Parking spaces!*** Good tyrants don't even own an umbrella. And why should they? They're not the ones who have to walk half a mile in the rain to get into the building.

- ***Closed-door meetings!*** Remember those doors I mentioned earlier? Well, here's a great way to put them to good use. Even if you're not talking about the deficiencies of everyone you didn't invite to your super-secret meeting, everyone on the other side of that door will have the opportunity to think that you are. Plus there's nothing like a highly publicized closed-door meeting to let your inferiors know that they aren't even important enough to know what changes might be affecting their own careers. Don't waste such a golden opportunity!

- ***Posting salary distinctions!*** Seriously, some companies do this. Need I say more?

- ***Never talking to anyone more than one pay grade below you!*** One of the most hallowed rules of tyrantdom is the understanding that those beneath you are congenitally incapable of saying anything worth hearing. After all, if they *did* have any decent ideas, they wouldn't be so far beneath you, would they? Huzzah for circular logic!

- ***Never answering your own phone!*** You are too important for such menial work. And if for any reason you aren't, then you definitely need to start acting like you are.
- ***Never scheduling your own meetings!*** See the above. This will be even more effective when your assistant is on an extended absence.

I could go on, of course - there are millions of techniques you can use. I'm sure you've discovered a few on your own. The important thing to keep in mind is that every good method of establishing positional dominance is designed to create a separation between you and the people beneath you. Some techniques are so subtle that your victims will question whether they're interpreting your actions correctly, while others are so blatant that they will function like a well-placed kick to the throat. But one thing will always be true:

The more techniques you use, the greater the separation – and the greater the separation, the more effective your blossoming tyranny will be.

Profiles in Tyranny: Larry Ellison

Larry Ellison is the co-founder of Oracle and one of the world's wealthiest men, a fact which he very much enjoys to make everyone else aware of at every opportunity. Case in point: in 2009 Ellison opened a conference for his own sales team and some of their biggest customers by first showing a 5-minute video of his personal sailboat, a 90-foot trimaran multi-hulled carbon fiber monstrosity so ridiculously customized that it wouldn't be surprising to learn that the ballast tanks are lumps of solid gold. It's said that Ellison had the sails of his 90-foot trimaran multi-hulled carbon fiber megaboat woven out of the skins of mermaids, which he had created in a genetics lab specifically for that purpose.

Anyway, at the end of the video, Larry Ellison walked onto the stage and *introduced* himself by saying, and I quote: "It's a great boat. You should get one."

Wow, Larry. Great advice. I'm pretty sure those things are still on clearance at Sears. Thanks for reminding me how much poorer I am than you. Can't wait to do more business with you.

Now it's possible that some of the techniques I've mentioned have been in effect in your workplace for as long as you can remember. It's also probable that some of them seem innocuous, ordinary and perfectly conventional. And that may be true – it's easy to put one or more of Chairman Jeff's techniques into practice without intending anything sinister. Happens all the time, in fact.

But it doesn't have to be that way.

The point, my aspiring tyrant, is that when it comes down to it, establishing positional dominance is all about intent. Of course you're going to have a higher salary and nicer things than someone who just started at your company a few days ago. That's totally normal. It's up to you, though, to make sure that your underlings *feel* inferior.

So if you have a door, make sure people *know* that you have a door. Get into the habit of opening and closing it often and loudly. If you have a privileged parking space, get a personalized license plate that says 'CLOSR' or 'SHRT WLK'. If you need to replace your all-leather captain's chair or mahogany desk, do it during the middle of the day when everybody you work with can see the moving people in action. Better yet, do it when your furniture doesn't actually need replacing. It's simple things like this, the sight of a perfectly gorgeous mahogany desk being removed from your office while another, identically gorgeous mahogany desk is being moved in, that will help create the kind of environment you should be striving to build.

Profiles in Tyranny: L. Dennis Kozlowski

Wow. If the former CEO of Tyco knew how to do anything at all, it was flaunt. Larry Ellison might have gone overboard by showing customers his personal sailboat, but at least a boat has a function. It moves across the water, transporting people from one place to the next. At the very least, a boat is something that people all around the world are interested in.

But there's really no way to justify spending $6,000 on a shower curtain or $15,000 on a 'dog umbrella stand'.

Except to show off how much money you're making, that is![3]

But those are personal possessions, and such things are hidden from view from the very *untermenschen* over whom you're trying to establish your positional dominance. It's not like Tyco employees are ever going to see the inside of your $30 million Manhattan home, are they Dennis? Of course not! So, what could an overpaid CEO do to really hammer home the size of his wallet? Certainly there's something more ostentatious than an expensive shower curtain?

Absolutely there is! How about hosting a $2 million birthday party for your wife on the island of Sardinia? (Tyco footed half of the bill for that, by the way, which is part of the reason that Mr. Kozlowski is currently in prison.) And, in a move that I must admit even I could never have thought of, he arranged for the centerpiece of the party to be an ice sculpture of David - specifically, an improved version of Michelangelo's original which urinated Stolichnaya vodka for thirsty guests. I can only assume that some kind of dessert was made available through the other end.

Pay careful attention, my aspiring tyrant. Until some CEO gets into the habit of arriving to work via Harrier jet, Mr. Kozlowski represents the absolute epitome of excess. You could learn a lot by following his example.

---

[3] It blows my mind that there is apparently a company out there that markets dog umbrella stands. How many of these can they possibly sell in a year? Because for $15,000, I could hire four people to hold a golden bowl above my dog to collect the rainwater. I could also hire someone to place embroidered towels along our entire walking route so that my furry little angel didn't have to suffer the indignity of wet paws.

Such as what the inside of a minimum-security prison looks like!

Now I know this example is probably beyond your abilities. You likely don't have several millions of dollars to waste in such extravagant fashion. But don't fear! There are plenty of ways you can establish your position dominance that won't cost you a penny.

Storytime!

Sandra H. was the department head at a civil service agency that provided services to families. She had been there for several years when a new Assistant Director came in, one that every aspiring tyrant could learn a lot from.

"Soon after our new Assistant Director began working in the agency, she called the Department leaders into a meeting and proudly proclaimed that she was able to get people fired from the previous agencies she had worked for," Sandra says. "She even bragged about getting a long-term employee fired because she didn't like him. She was very proud of this accomplishment and made sure we knew it! Then, following this meeting she proceeded to give a written reprimand to each one of us for some minor infraction. We decided that we were called into that meeting because we intimidated her and she wanted to send a message, that she was the one in charge."

Sounds like any tyrant's standard approach to establishing authority, right? But wait! There's more...

"This woman took every opportunity to rub her superiority into the faces of her employees. One time she showed up to work wearing jeans, which was not allowed, and when asked by a management team member why she was wearing jeans she replied, 'Because I can.'"

Living above the law, are we? Nothing unusual there. But wait! There's more...

"This woman tried to terminate a 10+ year exemplary employee for *hypothetical* infractions. The entire multiple page disciplinary document was filled with theoretical accusations – things the employee in question *might* have done wrong or *could have* done better. There was nothing concrete, and the firing was denied. So what did she do? She added six more 'what-if' infractions to the notice of discipline. The case went to appeal, and she lost again, because once again there was no proof of any wrongdoing. Not long after, the boss 'voluntarily left' the agency and went on to another agency to wreak her havoc."

Fantastic work, demon boss lady! Not only did you browbeat your employees into submission with your domineering presence and disdain for company policy – you also attempted to fire exemplary employees for no other reason than to exert your authority! There's a special place in Tyrant Heaven[4] for you.

---

[4] A lot of people call that place 'Hell,' but that's just because they know they'll never get to experience the glory of Tyrant Heaven.

My Personal Favorite

Of all the ways that you can establish positional dominance, there's one that stands head and shoulders above the rest. I created it (which of course is why it's the best technique there is), and it involves your standard, ordinary, run-of-the-mill organizational chart.

Now I'm sure you're all familiar with the org chart. Every company has one, even if yours is informal and unprinted. The org chart was initially designed to illustrate the relationship between various jobs within a given department or company. It's *supposed* to show employees how each job supports the organization as a whole, in much the same way that the body's organs combine in many remarkable ways to create a living being greater than the sum of its parts. And, if we extend the anatomical analogy just a little farther, the org chart can be said to have been designed to show that while some jobs and responsibilities may be more critical or visible than others, all are needed in order for the company to thrive and succeed.

Bollocks.[5]

Your org chart is the single greatest tool at your disposal to demonstrate, in a clear and undeniable way, how much better you are than the people you work with. And all it takes is one simple modification.

First, here's an example of an ordinary org chart. This might not exactly approximate the one that you're currently using, but you'll get the idea.

---

[5] That word is *way* underused, by the way. As is 'poppycock,' 'balderdash,' 'higgledy-piggledy,' and lots of others.

Example of Ineffective Org Chart

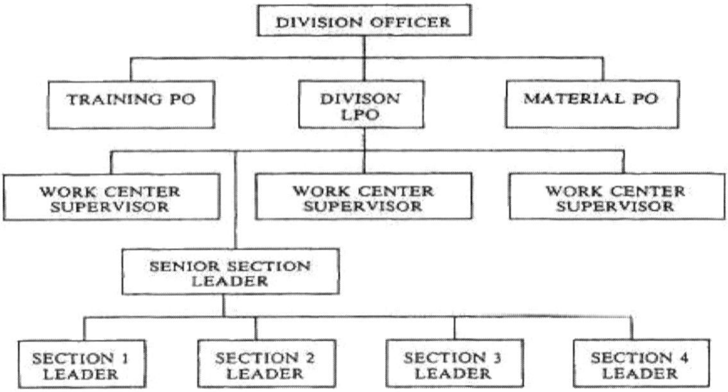

Now, for the modification. As I've said, it is very simple, but it conveys exactly the kind of message that a good tyrant should always be trying to convey:

Example of *Effective* Org Chart!

Heaven

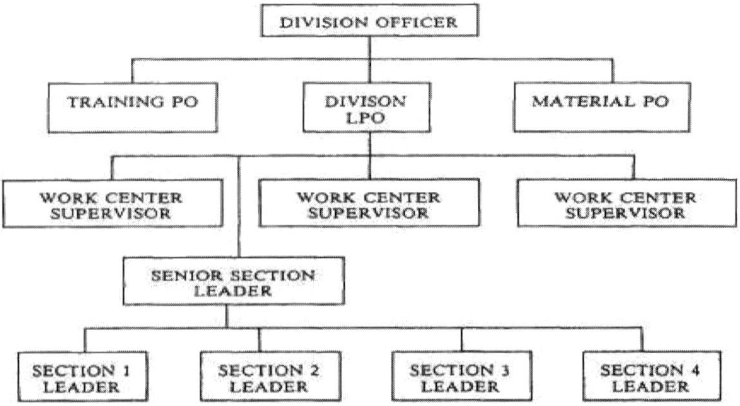

Hell

Hopefully you'll see the immediate applicability here. This will let your employees know exactly where they stand - not just in the company, but in the *world.* This simple addition to your org chart will let your inferiors know not only that you're above them in the company hierarchy, but that you're closer to perfection than they are - that they in turn are sinful and fallen, barely worth your august attention. I like to call these the Havens Holiness Lines. Make sure your org chart has them, and then pass a copy out to your employees on their first day of work. They need to know right from the beginning that you are better than them in every conceivable way: smarter, more interesting, wealthier, more important, a better dancer, a more capable Scrabble player - *everything.* A good tyrant always makes sure that those beneath him or her truly appreciate their status as peasants.

Storytime!

Claire was an assistant to a Hollywood producer. In general, production assistants are expected to do a little bit of everything - make phone calls, address envelopes, run errands, and all the thousand other duties that are required in the frenzied world of filmmaking. Claire's boss, however, took everything to an extreme.

"I could give you a thousand examples of how she treated me and everyone else who worked for her like dirt," Claire says.[6] "But here's one of my favorites. It was my job to check her out basket for things that needed doing. Well, one

[6] Most of the contributors to this book were quick to mention how many stories they could have shared, and more than a few were disappointed that they could only contribute one.

day my boss finished eating her lunch and put her used fork in her out-basket. I made the mistake of not picking it up. Half an hour later she walked by my desk, put her dirty fork in my inbox, leaned over my desk, and said, 'I put this in my out-basket for a reason.' I could have sworn my contract didn't say 'housekeeper' anywhere in it. Maybe I should have read it more carefully."

Congratulations, Hollywood producer! Your decision to constantly remind your employees of their status as indentured servants in your eyes will ensure that you always have a revolving door of new assistants to tyrannize. And nothing says productivity quite like having to train a new assistant every three months.

But What If I'm Not at the Top?

Seriously, do I have to do all of your thinking for you? This is not an issue. The chances of you being at the top of your org chart are slim – after all, there can be only one top dog. But just because you're not at the top doesn't mean you can't *look* like you're at the top.

Let me show you what I mean. Look at the next page. Now, let's imagine that this is your company's org chart. You are a senior section leader, and your position is indicated by the series of exclamation points I've placed next to your title to make you feel more impressive than you deserve to feel. To be honest, I'm disappointed that you haven't climbed higher, but since we're at the beginning of the book, I'm holding out some hope that you'll soon be moving up.

Example of Full Org Chart

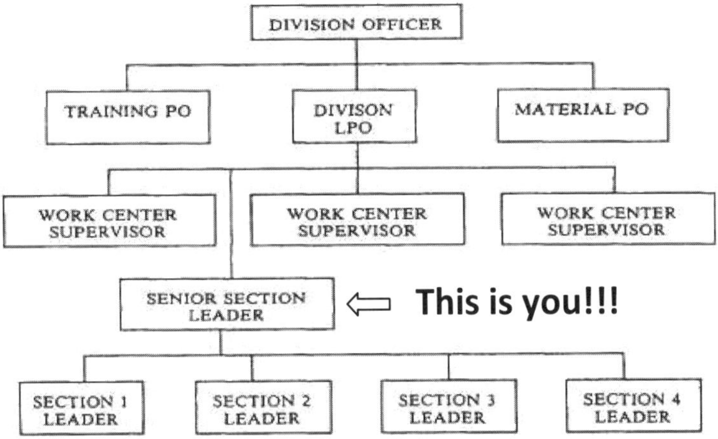

That's where you belong. But there's really no reason to show your employees the entire company org chart, is there? Especially when doing so will not make you seem dominant and supreme. So just show them what they need to see.

Example of Properly Modified Org Chart

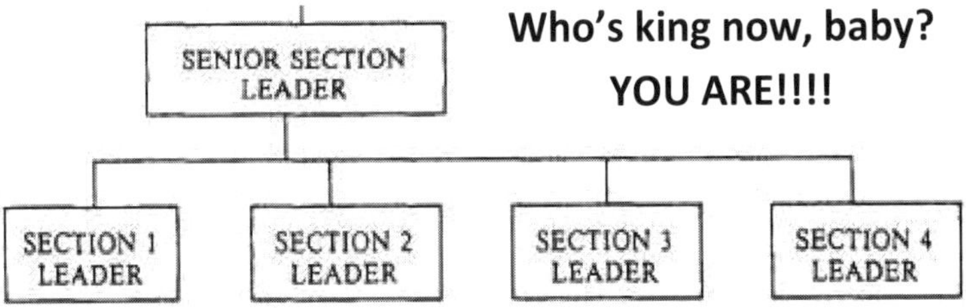

Easy enough, right? Instead of looking like a middle manager, you've given yourself the appearance of supremacy. Quick, easy, effective – and most importantly, tyrannical.

So, once you've positioned yourself above the Neanderthals you're forced to share an office with, it's time to move on.

…

…

…

What are you waiting for? Turn the page, idiot. Let's move on.

Create Grandiloquent Titles for Yourself!

"Her Majesty Elizabeth the Second, by the Grace of God, of Great Britain, Ireland and the British Dominions beyond the Seas Queen, Defender of the Faith, Duchess of Edinburgh, Countess of Merioneth, Baroness Greenwich, Duke of Lancaster, Lord of Mann, Duke of Normandy, Sovereign of the Most Honourable Order of the Garter, Sovereign of the Most Honourable Order of the Bath, Sovereign of the Most Ancient and Most Noble Order of the Thistle, Sovereign of the Most Illustrious Order of Saint Patrick, Sovereign of the Most Distinguished Order of Saint Michael and Saint George, Sovereign of the Most Excellent Order of the British Empire, Sovereign of the Distinguished Service Order, Sovereign of the Imperial Service Order, Sovereign of the Most Exalted Order of the Star of India, Sovereign of the Most Eminent Order of the Indian Empire, Sovereign of the Order of British India, Sovereign of the Indian Order of Merit, Sovereign of the Order of Burma, Sovereign of the Royal Order of Victoria and Albert, Sovereign of the Royal Family Order of King Edward VII, Sovereign of the Order of Merit, Sovereign of the Order of the Companions of Honour, Sovereign of the Royal Victorian Order, Sovereign of the Most Venerable Order of the Hospital of St John of Jerusalem."

Official Title of Queen Elizabeth II,
upon her ascension to the British throne

So, you've positioned yourself properly, above the peons that scurry and scamper among the cubicles outside your imposing office wall. They know who's boss - or at least, they know that you've told them who the boss is. But if there's any axiom that you should get in the habit of following, it's this one:

If you really want your employees to know who the boss is, you'll need to beat it into their heads in as many ways as possible

Enter the subject of this chapter - creating grandiloquent titles for yourself. The best titles are long, flowery, and have almost no relevance to the person whose titles they are *except* as a way to separate yourself from those beneath you. A good title is like an expensive diamond - intrinsically useless but still a symbol of your affluence and importance.

Oh, and there's one more similarity between titles and diamonds: the more you have, the happier you'll be. So let's hurry up and get you that tennis bracelet you've always wanted, shall we?

Avoiding Frivolous or Amusing Titles

The use of titles to signify rank and importance has a long and illustrious history, and is most notably visible in the militaries of every country in the known universe. Every promotion comes with a change in title, and every new title demands a greater level of respect and deference.

However, there is a significant difference between military titles and corporate titles; specifically, military titles *must* be earned. A person must spend more time and energy to become a brigadier general than, say, a sergeant. In the corporate world, though, titles *might* be earned but can also be conferred for no reason whatsoever.

The fact that corporate titles can be given to anyone for any reason has occasionally led to a medical condition known as Fancy Title Madness, in which frivolous and amusing titles are given to every employee at every level in the organization. I've seen business cards with titles such as "CEO and Princess," "Web Ninja," "IT Super-Guru," "President and Chief Jedi," and dozens more. Perhaps your organization has engaged in this practice. Perhaps you even think it's cute.

But if you're hoping to become a successful tyrant, there are two problems to this approach. The first is that when you give fancy titles to everyone, they lose their tyrannical power. You need to have *more* and *better* titles than those beneath you – otherwise, how will they ever come to fear you?

The other problem with frivolous titles is that the companies who use them often do so as a sign of solidarity and shared commitment to the cause. I shouldn't have to say this, but I'm going to anyway: *avoid this at all costs.* There are few things worse to your career as a tyrant than for your subordinates to feel a kinship to you. Not to mention that the proliferation of such titles generally suggests a fun and laid-back working atmosphere. Is that what you're going for? Absolutely not! Fear, self-interest, and mistrust - those are your goals. So as entertaining as it might be for people to refer to you as the "Lead Guitarist of Human Resources," resist the urge. There are better, more diabolical choices to consider.

The Right Way to Do It

There are three ways to create grandiloquent titles for yourself that are in keeping with your goal of unleashing your inner tyrant. The first, and simplest, is to give yourself titles that speak directly to your superiority. Kim Jong-Il, for example, is the "Supreme Leader"; Octavius Augustus called himself *princeps*, or "First Citizen." Other possible options include *Honorable, Venerable, His/Her Excellency, The Majestic* - you get the idea. I could go on, of course, but I don't think either of us wants this chapter to be 4,000 pages long.

A second, more inventive approach is to accept titles from your subordinates - that is, force them to bestow titles upon you - that are obsequious in their flattery. One of the best examples of this approach is Joseph Stalin, who is the subject of our next Profile in Tyranny.

Profiles in Tyranny: Joseph Stalin

A tyrant in every sense of the word, Joseph Stalin presided over the Soviet Union from 1924 until his death in 1953. His death, incidentally, was most likely caused by poisoning, since he fell unexpectedly ill after a dinner and his immediate

subordinates waited more than a day to call for a doctor. Just thought you might want to know.

Anyway, most of the techniques Stalin used to tyrannize his subordinates - murder, extortion, ransomed kidnappings, bloody purges, sham trials, impromptu executions, state-sanctioned genocide, etc. - are probably not transferrable to your particular business. Seriously, the guy was ruthless; he actually quit the Bolshevik Party for a short time because they had the nerve to outlaw bank robberies, which Stalin was apparently a big fan of carrying out. But his penchant for grandiose titles is definitely something you can learn from.

Stalin's first title was one he gave himself: Stalin. His birth name was Ioseb Besarionis dze Jughashvili, which doesn't exactly roll off the tongue. So he changed it to Stalin, both for ease of use and because it is the Russian word for 'steel.'

However, his best titles were those that were given to him during his long reign of terror atop the Soviet throne. Stalin accepted such titles as Brilliant Genius of Humanity (patently absurd), Coryphaeus of Science (incomprehensible), and my personal favorite, Gardener of Human Happiness, which would have been laughable if laughing at it wouldn't have gotten you killed. Collectively these titles helped Stalin craft a cult of personality that, along with his other acts of tyranny, helped him become one of the 20th century's most successful and long-lasting tyrants.

Until he was poisoned, that is.

The example of Joseph Stalin should make you realize two things. First, the best tyrants have a handful of elaborate titles tucked away, ready for use at a moment's notice either to impress a possible client or to make the process of introducing them at a state dinner long enough for the soup to thoroughly cool. And second, if you plan on really taking the lessons of this book to heart, you might want to invest in a poison taster. There are plenty of college students that would probably be up for the job.

Before we get into the third technique for creating grandiloquent titles, let's see how these first two can work together. Below is an example of a typical business card

Ordinary Business Card

Bob Bobson
Associate project manager, digital content
General Amalgamated Industries, Inc.
555-555-5555 – office
555-555-5556 – fax
bobbobson@generalamal.com

This card, in a word, is boring. Bland, ordinary, tepid, banal - however you want to describe it, this is the business card of a colorless and ineffectual functionary. And while you might try to doll it up with fancy graphics, typefaces, and shapes - I recently saw a business card shaped like the Eiffel Tower, which is weird since the guy who gave it to me refused to sell me the Eiffel Tower - no matter what cosmetic touches you include, the fact remains that this is the uninspiring business card of an uninspiring person.

However, with a few grandiloquent titles thrown in, even the most ordinary of business cards can become amazing.

Extraordinary Business Card!

His Excellency, The Right Honorable and Pusillanimous **Bob Bobson** Sage, Ayatollah, Project Czar, Grandmaster of the Internet Father of Thought, First Among Unequals, Great Doer of All Things Worth Doing General Amalgamated Industries, Inc. 555-555-5555 – office 555-555-5556 – fax bobthesupreme@generalamal.com

I trust you can see the difference. *This* is the business card of an important person, someone who not only demands respect but who will attempt to throttle it out of you in the very act of handing you his or her contact information. The more of these kinds of titles you can think to give yourself, the more important it will make you feel, and the more annoying it will be to everyone else. Because nothing says 'pretentious windbag' quite like a business card filled with titles and phrases that mean nothing to anybody but the person whose card it is.[1]

Now I know many of you will be reluctant to take the bold leap that I've just suggested. Perhaps you don't know what an 'ayatollah' is and don't want to look stupid when somebody asks about it, or perhaps you're afraid this kind of grandiloquent overkill will make you look absurd rather than

[1] Also, please note the change in email addresses, a small yet important detail that will remind people of your importance and power every time they are forced to write you.

tyrannical. Personally, I disagree. I can't think of a more domineering word than 'czar,' and believe me I've tried. What would you rather be – project manager, or project czar? The choice should be obvious.

However, if you'd like to dip your toes into the water before diving all the way in, there is the third way I mentioned earlier. It is the easiest approach, as it will require absolutely no creativity on your part, and it's a path that I'm happy to say many businesspeople have already taken – and that is, to include on your business card every conceivable award, acronym, and educational degree you've ever earned. This approach has the advantage of being an already common practice, not to mention that you will have legitimately earned all of the superlatives you'll be printing.

Here's an example:

Actual Business Card I Got at a Conference Once (name has been changed)

Dr. Harold Darbleganger,
M.Ed., J.D., Ph.D., CPLA
Phi Beta Kappa
Software Solutions, Inc.
555-555-5555 – office
555-555-5556 – fax
hdarbleganger@softsolutions.com

I think we got it, Mr. Darbleganger – you went to a lot of school. Thanks for letting the entire world know how much smarter you are than the rest of us. Phi Beta Kappa, I see – very impressive. Does that have any bearing on your abilities as a software engineer? Absolutely not. And yet you felt compelled to share it with me. Thanks.

As you can tell, this business card annoyed me. But of course, that's exactly what you should be shooting for. A good tyrant wastes no opportunity to make the people he or she meets feel inferior. If you're really good at this, the text on your business card should wrap around to the back side.

Also, these days it costs less than $20 to get 1,000 business cards printed, an absolute steal considering the return you'll receive. So what are you waiting for? Just because your company hasn't authorized new business cards for you does *not* mean that you should wait. So get something grandiose and obnoxious off to the printers this instant! Because after all, impatience is another hallmark of a successful tyrant.

Bonus Time! Titles as Subjugation

But wait, my aspiring tyrant – there's more! It should now be obvious that the creation of absurdly elaborate titles, awards, designations, and other honorifics can help convey a sense of your own inflated importance. However, it's also true that titles can be used as a subtle and nefarious weapon against your subordinates.

How, you ask? Simple – by giving elaborate titles to everyone!

On first glance, this might seem counter-intuitive, not to mention a direct contradiction to my earlier injunction to avoid handing out frivolous and amusing titles. But it isn't. First off, the titles I'm talking about here should not be frivolous or amusing; that would indeed be a bad idea, as it might create a warm and friendly bond between you and your employees, which of course is a relationship you need to avoid like the plague. Rather, the titles I'm talking about should look like a serious attempt on your part to add a little extra dignity and panache to your employees' jobs.

"But wait," you must be thinking. "If I give them impressive-sounding titles, won't they start to feel more impressive?"

It's possible. They might indeed start to feel better about themselves.

But not if their title comes with absolutely no tangible rewards!

Therein lies the true genius of this technique. Titles are generally viewed as a way to bestow a sense of importance. But if the title is the *only* thing you're giving to someone…well, that's generally seen as an empty gesture, a cheap and transparent attempt to soothe unhappy workers without providing them with anything of value. You know that, *they* know that – but most importantly, *they know that you know that!!!*

And I'm pleased to be able to announce that this is happening all the time. In the last few years companies and managers across the world have 'promoted' people without offering them any of the perks of promotion. "Account Executives" have become "Brand Management Excellence Coordinators." "Project Managers" have become "Senior Portfolio Managers," then "Senior Portfolio Excellence Managers," then "Lead Senior Portfolio Excellence Supervising Managers." Same job, same pay, same level of responsibility – different title.

The important thing, of course, is to make sure that *your* added titles also come with some added perk – extra pay, better benefits, stock options, etc. – but that *your employees'* added titles do not. It's this disparity, the fact that your titles mean something while theirs don't, that will best help you unleash your inner tyrant through the use of grandiloquent titles.

Now I know you're anxious to keep reading. But before you turn the page, do yourself a favor. Spend 10 or 15 minutes thinking up an appropriately incredible series of titles for yourself, then call your engraver and order a new nameplate for your office door. Sure, he might have to work through the weekend to get your order completed, but it will be a nice treat for you when you walk into the office on Monday.

Dressing Like An Autocrat

"I wear expensive suits. They just look cheap on me."
Warren Buffett

You know what's so unfortunate about the quote above? That it's true. Warren Buffett's suits *do* look cheap on him. And you know what else? Nobody has ever called Warren Buffett a tyrant. The most savvy investor in the history of modern American business, yes; witty and oddly charming, certainly; an interesting dancer, undoubtedly. But not a tyrant. And part of the reason for that is the way he carries himself.

Which is why you need to pay careful attention to this chapter. If you want to act like a tyrant, it will help you to look like one.

Do you *need* to dress like a tyrant? Strictly speaking, no. You don't need to, just like you don't need to visit Greece, or have multiple vacation homes, or own a 300-foot pleasure yacht, or hide your money in Swiss tax shelters. But it sure is nice to. So instead of wasting my time with stupid questions, why don't we keep things moving along, OK?

When it comes to professional attire, the sad truth is that most of us dress alike regardless of position. Chances are you're not wearing a terribly expensive outfit as you're reading this. And even if you are, most people can't tell the difference between expensive and inexpensive clothing. A casual glance will not tell me if your suit cost $200 or $2,000 – and that is unacceptable.

Like it or not, your personal appearance is the first thing people notice about you. And if they can tell at a glance how expensive your car or home is, they should be able to discern the same thing from the clothes and other accoutrements that you wear into the office. And right now they probably can't.

How did things get to such a sorry state? There was a time in this country when men and women of every professional stripe dressed to impress. Men wore sharp hats and three-piece suits, women wore crisp dresses, and everybody ironed everything, including their shoes. And then one day that era vanished, replaced by a workforce whose members often look like they're heading to a carnival or backyard kegger rather than on their way toward something productive.

What happened? The answer can be found in these two words:

Casual. Friday.

Encourage a 'Casual Friday' Mentality

In order to understand how you can use Casual Friday to your tyrannical advantage, it will first help you to understand where the phenomenon came from.

History Time! – Casual Friday

After World War II, the American workplace was flooded with returning soldiers eager for a return to normalcy

and happy to take whatever jobs they were offered. They worked hard, lived modestly, and dressed as though work were the most important part of their lives – because in many cases, it was. As a result, the late 1940s and early 1950s represents the era in which the average worker's average working outfit was at its most impressive.

By the 1950s, however, the postwar enthusiasm for working life had largely faded. Work had once again become the slow, inexorable drain on joy that it is today. Productivity began to taper off, and so company CEOs cast about for ways to improve worker morale. After discarding such radical ideas as 'better pay' and 'more comfortable working environments,' they finally settled on one of America's most hallowed modern customs: Casual Friday, where workers were encouraged to go crazy one day a week and wear comfortable clothes.

By the 1970s the tradition was firmly entrenched, and by the 1990s Casual Friday had become Casual Everyday. Workers eschewed suits and ties for T-shirts and sandals. Frayed seams, spaghetti straps, and words plastered across the backside became a common sight. In a scant few decades the American workplace began to look more like a college campus than a theater of business.

Today, the term 'Casual Friday' has largely disappeared. In a way, it is a victim of its own success. Average workers are now so casual in their dress that encouraging them to dress more casually on Friday would require them to show up naked. And while there are a very small number of businesses where nudity is the preferred attire, in most cases it is a really, really, *really* bad idea.

Did Casual Friday make people any happier? Of course not. But it wasn't supposed to. It was designed as a way for workers to forget their private sorrow, to encourage them to ignore their self-imposed misery by allowing them to rack their tiny brains every morning over which tube top to wriggle into. It is a very subtle method of control.

Whether we realize it or not, our self-perception is influenced by the way we carry ourselves. Dress a beggar like a king, and eventually he will begin to view himself as a king. And if your subordinates dress as though they are subordinate to you, then they will ever-so-subtly begin to feel that subordination.

Which of course is why you need to encourage a 'Casual Friday' mentality in your workforce. The more slovenly they dress, the more you should praise their choices. This is one of the only methods in the entire *Unleash Your Inner Tyrant!* program that will cause your employees to thank you for what you're doing. They might even compliment you on your willingness to let them express themselves through their wardrobe. They'll believe you're giving them freedom.

And you are. The freedom to put themselves in an inferior position to you, that is.

Avoid the 'Casual Friday' Mentality!

Now I've already alluded to this, but in the interest of beating you over the head with the obvious, I'm going to spell it out: under no circumstances should you allow yourself to adopt a 'Casual Friday' mentality. Your problem – well, one of your many problems – is that you have probably allowed yourself to be infected by this dangerous line of thinking.

Perhaps you've gotten in the habit of taking your tie off an hour after arriving to work because it constricts your ability to breathe easily. Perhaps you've worn a football jersey to work the Friday before the Super Bowl. You might even have allowed yourself to fall so far as to wear sneakers with your three-piece suit because they're more comfortable than dress shoes – and besides, who sees your feet when you're sitting behind your desk anyway?

Listen up, my aspiring tyrant – *tyrants do not wear sneakers.* They don't even own sneakers. Sneakers are for people who are trying to hide from others. Sneakers are for people who play racquetball and enjoy lazy days in the park. Tyrants, on the other hand, wear hard and unyielding shoes, the kind that echo sharply against the uncarpeted floors of your office. The kind of shoes that herald your approach from a quarter mile off, the kind of shoes designed to deliver maximum damage whenever you choose to deliver a swift kick to the backsides of your subordinates. Are we clear?

The point is, while your employees may indulge in a Casual Friday mentality, you may not. You never saw a picture of Saddam Hussein in a track suit, did you? I think not. And Al Dunlap never wore Zubaz while he was firing thousands of Sunbeam workers and driving that company into the ground.[1] The greater the disconnect between what you wear and what your employees wear, the greater the separation. And as I've said before, the greater the separation, the more effective your tyranny will be.

So, let's start small before we really get going, shall we?

---

[1] More on Al Dunlap's particular skills as a tyrant in a later chapter.

Dressing Like an Autocrat – Beginners

- ***Cufflinks*** Why use buttons when you can accomplish the same thing with an expensive pair of cufflinks?
- ***Shiny tone-on-tone suits*** Those few of your subordinates who bother wearing suits will probably opt for either a simple monochrome affair or a subtle pinstripe. Shiny tone-on-tone suits, however, have two advantages. They are visibly more expensive than the rags your employees are wearing, and their shininess (as well as their tone-on-tone-iness) make them oddly hypnotic. Seriously, I once captured the attention of a random passerby who got caught staring at my shiny tone-on-tone suit and ended up convincing him to mow my lawn for me.
- ***Tie clips*** For somebody who is going to be yelling at underlings as much as you will be, the tie clip is more than just a smart piece of wardrobe propaganda – it will also keep your tie from flailing about and making you look disheveled and unprofessional as you're ranting and raving. The perfect blend of form and function.
- ***Any designer anything (bags, purses, watches, etc.) with the designer's name prominently displayed*** This will require a bit more work on your part, since many of your subordinates are likely to have cheap imitations of designer goods. But

what's the point of owning a $500 purse that looks exactly like a $20 knockoff if you don't make a point of talking about how much you spent on yours?

- ***French cuffs***, which they don't even wear in France. Are you going to a wedding? Nope, just sending a not-so-subtle signal to your worker bees that you make more money than they do. Mission accomplished.

- ***The Double Windsor knot***, which only seven people on Earth know how to tie. Those seven live alone, communing with nature on the tops of hard-to-reach mountains. Seek them out. Bring them hot tea, yak's blood, and a small sacrifice. Only then will they divulge their secrets.

Now I know some of you have been working on these ideas for years. I've heard of businessmen calling the concierge at their hotel with a full-blown cufflink crisis because they left their own at home and the idea of going to tomorrow's meeting without cufflinks was simply too horrifying to contemplate.

But these ideas are just the tip of the iceberg. If you want to follow in the footsteps of the some of the world's most successful tyrants, you'll need to go above and beyond the ordinary. When it comes to your wardrobe, you shouldn't *suggest* or *hint at* your supremacy; you need to beat your subordinates over the head with a hammer – or, in your case, with an overly expensive attaché.

So, if you'd like to leave the wading pool and dive into the deep end with the rest of the big boys and girls, here are some more ideas for you to consider:

Dressing Like an Autocrat – Advanced

- ***Capes*** Nothing is quite as regal, as majestic, or as awe-inspiring as a quality cape. It will lend you the aura of a superhero or vampire king, and it is constantly dramatic. Plus, nobody else has one, which should be reason enough for you to get one for yourself.
- ***A crown or tiara*** After all, you *are* the most important person in the office, right? The de facto king or queen of your realm? Then make it official.
- ***A scepter*** Did I say that nothing was as regal or majestic or awe-inspiring as a cape? Well, I was lying. There is something more awesome than a cape, and it's called a scepter. Because not only is it an unquestionable symbol of your dominance, it can also be used as a weapon. Puts Harry Cohn's riding crop to shame.
- ***The top hat/monacle combo*** If your flavor of tyranny is more robber baron than divine monarch, this is definitely the way to go. You'll probably want to take up cigar smoking as well, and get in the habit of blowing your cigar smoke in other people's faces.

- ***Medals*** Usually reserved for generals-turned-military-dictators, there is no reason why you can't inaugurate the tradition in your corporate environment. Napoleon had medals out the wazoo, and he didn't even have indoor plumbing. And if you don't have a sycophantic sidekick willing to pin them on for you, do it yourself! All the best tyrants have, and there's no reason to mess with their winning system.

The point is, you shouldn't want to dress like your subordinates, any more than you should want to spend time with them or get to know their names.

But I'm getting ahead of myself. The last several chapters should have taught you how to create a separation between you and the people who work for you. We're going to move now into a discussion of how to utilize that separation to the greatest effect. So far we've focused almost exclusively on self-interest, and now it's time to delve into the fear and mistrust. Lots of good stuff to come!

But before we do, I have a little surprise for you. Bonus section time!!!!

Sucking Like a Champion!

Delivering an Ineffective Powerpoint Presentation

Hello, and welcome to the first installment of *Sucking Like a Champion!* I'd like to take a moment to congratulate those of you who are actually reading this, since it's listed as a 'bonus' chapter and thus not strictly necessary for your education. Your above-and-beyond dedication to becoming a thoroughly deplorable leader is nothing short of extraordinary, and I salute you.

So, why have I included these sections? Well, this book is the brainchild of a corporate presentation I've been delivering for years to businesses and government entities across North America. And in the process of talking to all of these different businesspeople, I realized a couple important points:

a) The title *Unleash Your Inner Tyrant!* is totally awesome and way better than anything else I came up with.[1]

---

[1] A sampling of my discarded titles: *Principles of Ineffective Leadership* (so boring I almost fell asleep writing just those four words); *The Angry Pineapple* (great for a children's story or childlike business parable, but a little less forceful than I wanted); *Crushing the Child Within* (a little dark even for me); and *What Would Richard Fuld Do?*

b) Despite the obvious truth of the previous statement, there are several ways to create a toxic, unfulfilling, counterproductive, and otherwise imperfect working environment that are not necessarily tyrannical in nature.

Hence the need for *Sucking Like a Champion!* This and subsequent *Sucking* sections will focus on various ways to make the ordinary operation of your business as drab, colorless, monotonous, uninspiring, and tedious as possible. If you take the time to read every *Sucking Like a Champion!* offering, then you'll learn far more than how to be an effective tyrant. You'll also learn how to take all of the joy out of some of the most common of business practices.

Please understand, *you do not have to be a tyrant in order to do this.* In fact, most of the people who engage in *Sucking* behaviors are not tyrants. They are well-meaning individuals who manage nevertheless to do a really bad job at certain things. But since these well-meaning folks have discovered a few excellent ways to make work seem like a prison sentence, you should definitely attempt to make the advice in each *Sucking* section an integral part of your working model.

This first installment will teach you how to create and deliver the kind of lackluster Powerpoint presentation that will make even the most courteous members of your workforce tune you out completely. You will have undoubtedly seen some of these techniques in Powerpoint presentations you've had to suffer through in the past, so this should be a fairly easy lesson.

Are you ready? I actually don't care if you are or not, because I'm going to continue anyway. So let's get started!

- **Step One:** Make sure that your presentation is created by somebody with absolutely no expertise in graphic design. In many cases this person will be you, but many of you will delegate it to any number of your computer-illiterate underlings. Now perhaps you're thinking, "Why should design matter? It's not the way it looks but rather the material being presented that's important." And if that's what you're thinking, congratulations! Not only have you already mastered this step, but you've done so in a way that runs contrary to every natural human instinct. You probably live in a house completely devoid of color and decoration, wear the same ill-fitting clothes every day, and would have been perfectly happy if you had never laid eyes on your spouse prior to the day of your marriage. The point is, your insistence that design has no bearing on perception places you in a world so full of denial that the rest of the *Unleash Your Inner Tyrant!* program should come to you as naturally as breathing.
- **Step Two:** After you've created a dowdy and unappealing suite of fonts and backgrounds for your Powerpoint, make sure that everything you plan on saying – every sentence, and ideally every word – is displayed in the Powerpoint itself. This accomplishes two things. First, it saves you the trouble of having to prepare yourself before the presentation. If you ever forget what you're going to say, you can always

kill the flow of your presentation with an awkward pause as you scan your own Powerpoint to remember your own major points. But more importantly, this technique also ensures that everyone you're presenting to *knows* that you didn't prepare yourself. And as soon as your audience gets the subtle but distinct impression that the information you're presenting isn't even important enough for *you* to know what it is, they'll begin the inexorable process of ignoring you.

- **Step Three:** Display your information in paragraph-sized chunks. It is an unspoken rule among professional speakers – and by 'unspoken' I mean 'widely publicized and freely shared' – that every click of your wireless pointer should add no more than six to ten words of text to a given Powerpoint slide, and that a full slide should contain no more than six lines of text. But I see no reason why you should listen to the advice of people who deliver animated and engaging presentations for a living. So display 50 words at a time! If your slide has six major points, don't display each point as you plan to discuss it – display all six points at once! The best of you will actually reduce the point size of your text in order to cram more information into a given slide, which will make it impossible for the people sitting in the back to actually see whatever it is you're displaying. More importantly, though, most of us automatically read whatever we see, and most of us can read a given paragraph much faster than the average person can say it aloud. So the more text you display at any one time, the more likely it is that your audience will immediately focus on reading each slide as quickly as possible so they can go back to playing Tetris on their iPhones. Plus, the act of reading a paragraph at one speed while somebody else says it aloud at a slightly different speed is just plain annoying, and you'd be foolish to overlook such a golden opportunity to irritate your audience.

- **Step Four (the final and most important step):** Provide printed copies of your Powerpoint to everyone in attendance *before* you start talking. A good leader might provide an outline to his or her audience at the end of a presentation, which can be frustrating - after all, if there's anything the average professional needs, it's *more paper*! - but which does have the undeniable benefit of helping to reinforce the major points that have just been presented. However, if you want to suck like a champion, you will give your audience as many ways to ignore you as possible. And while you might think it helpful to provide an outline of your upcoming presentation before you start talking, a printout actually causes people to believe that everything that might be even slightly important will be printed right there for them - after all, if the person giving the presentation didn't bother to write something down, how important could it be? Most audience members will quickly scan through a printed Powerpoint presentation, absorb what they believe are the main points, and then tune out for the duration of the actual presentation itself. Plus, providing people with a few sheets of paper gives them something to draw on when they're bored – how thoughtful of you!

So there you have it. There are other techniques to consider that will help you ruin what could otherwise have been an interesting and productive Powerpoint – talking in the soul-crushing monotone that Ben Stein uses to such delicious effect, attaching audio samples to the wrong slides, forgetting to change the batteries on your wireless clicker before you begin, overusing animation and other special effects, displaying too many charts and graphs at the same time, using *any* puns whatsoever, etc. – but this should get you started.

Hope you enjoyed your little break. Now, let's get back to business!

Remain Aloof and Above

"The Depression is good for the country.
The only problem is that it might not last long enough,
in which case people might not learn enough from it."
Henry Ford

"If the peasants have no bread, then let them eat cake."
Marie Antoinette[1]

So, you've established your unconquerable authority. You've solidified your claims with the appropriate titles, and you're dressing better than you ever have before. By now you should be feeling pretty good about yourself.

Your question now should be, "So, what do I *do* with all of this?"

Easy. You've *positioned* yourself above your subordinates. Now it's time to *operate* above them as well.

---

[1] Odds are she never actually said this. It was probably invented by her enemies during the French Revolution in order to demonstrate her ignorance of and indifference to the plight facing the starving peasantry, which was then used to justify her capture and execution. But it's a good quote, and it serves the purposes of this chapter, so I'm using it. Who cares if it's accurate? This book is called *Unleash Your Inner Tyrant!*, not *Unleash Your Inner Fact-Checker!*. Besides, we'll be discussing how to deal with the truth and other inconveniences in a later chapter. So for all you self-righteous history majors scoffing at my possible misquotation, just consider this a preview of what's to come.

You are the brains of your company or division, the animating force behind everything good that happens. Your employees, to continue the anatomical analogy, are the feet, the engine that powers your company or division. And your brain doesn't have to see your feet in order to tell them what to do, does it? Of course not! In fact, your brain is located in your head specifically so that it can stay as far away from your feet as possible.

I think I've made my point. Your employees are like feet. Disgusting, stinky feet. So take a page from your brain's playbook, and remain aloof and above. Because no good tyrant ever, *ever* smells like feet.

Forget Everything You've Ever Read, Heard, Thought, or Thought about Thinking

For some of you, the mandates of this chapter are going to come very easily. You've never liked the people you've worked with, never respected their abilities or felt that you had anything in common with them. Your eyes have always glazed over when your direct reports have started in about their boring hopes and dreams – or worse, shared stories about their children. If that describes you, then this will all seem natural. Just make sure you lock your office door behind you so that you can read this without anybody interrupting you to ask an important question or invite you to lunch.

For most of you, though, this will be a significant departure from what you've read in other books. The vast majority of management and leadership literature sings the praises of knowing your employees, the supposed benefits that accrue from creating a culture where managers and their employees spend time together. They'll cite statistics such as the following:

- In a 25-year Gallup study of 80,000 employees and managers, the single greatest determiner of an employee's longevity and productivity was found to be the employee's relationship with his immediate supervisor.

- A study by the Anderson Consulting Group's Institute for Strategic Change found that the cumulative stock price of companies that were perceived to be well led grew 900% over a ten-year period, versus 74% in companies that were perceived to be lacking in effective leadership.

- A Dutch survey found that the average life expectancy of all businesses in 12.5 years, and the average life expectancy of multinational corporations (Fortune 500 or equivalent) is between 40 and 50 years. One-third of companies registered on the Fortune 500 in the 1970s had disappeared by 1983. Arie de Geus, author of *Living Company,* blames such rampant failure on the focus of managers on profits and the bottom line rather than the human community that makes up their organization.

- According to the U.S. Department of Labor, the most common reason people leave their jobs is because "they do not feel appreciated".

Some of these books even go so far as to highlight examples of particular executives who have adopted a 'Know Your Employees' philosophy:

- George Zimmer, founder and CEO of Men's Wearhouse, has made it a personal crusade to have as much face time with his employees as possible. He personally trained many of his stores' entry-level sales associates long after he needed to be the one doing so, and he attends over 20 Men's Wearhouse holiday parties around the country every year and even dances with his employees.

- Herb Kelleher, Southwest's longtime President and CEO, was famous for occasionally throwing bags on the tarmac with the other baggage handlers. And in 1994, Southwest's employees spent $60,000 of their own money to take out a full-page ad in USA Today on Boss's Day to thank Herb for, among other things, remembering all of their names.

And have these approaches been successful? That all depends on how you define success. Men's Wearhouse, for example, boasts a 10% employee turnover ratio compared to an industry average of 25.1%, and as of 2004 George Zimmer's 8.7% stake in the company he founded was worth an estimated $94 million. And as for Southwest, Fortune magazine regularly lists it as one of the top five Most Admired Companies in America, and during his tenure Herb Kelleher produced the highest return to shareholders of any company in the S&P 500. I suppose there are some people who would consider these examples of success.

But not me.

Take my word on this: neither George Zimmer, Herb Kelleher, nor anybody else who follows their management philosophies has ever had the honor of being called a tyrant. You do not want to end up like these two, adored by your subordinates and praised in the pages of gossip rags like *Fortune* magazine. But you will if you do as they've done.

Why You Should Avoid Contact With Your Employees

I'm embarrassed that I feel the need to write this section. It should be obvious why you need to avoid your employees as much as possible, just like it should be obvious why you occasionally need to fill you car with gasoline or tell your children that they won't always look as bad as they do when puberty strikes. But *Unleash Your Inner Tyrant!* wouldn't be a real management and leadership book if I didn't beat you over the head with a few obvious truths, so here goes.

The most readily apparent reason to remain aloof and above is this:

Other people are annoying

If you remember only one sentence out of this entire book, it should be that one. Other people are annoying. They always have been. In fact, they've been annoying you for as long as you can remember: making fun of you on the school bus, writing checks at the grocery store checkout – seriously, people, join the 1980s and *get yourself a debit card!!!!* – and don't even get me started on slow drivers clogging up the passing lane. It is primarily because other people are so annoying that we live in separate homes. It is because other people are annoying that our offices are separated by walls or carpeted partitions, so that we can spend as little time with each other as possible.

And you are not exempt from this. I'm sure the act of eating dinner with you (whoever you are, and I hope I never find out) is like pulling teeth.

If you ever need any actual proof that other people are annoying, here's all you need to do: the next time you have 10 minutes to kill, scroll through all the contacts in your cell phone. I'm certain that you have several numbers in there for people you never call. What's more, if those people call you, you often hit 'ignore' and let it go to voicemail. Why? Because you don't want to talk to them. And why is that? *Because they're annoying*. And those are *friends,* theoretically. Those are people you exchanged business cards with, people to whom you said, "Give me your number, let's keep up."

The point is, if you have *friends* you don't want to talk to because they're annoying, it's safe to say you work with people that you find even more intolerable. The prosecution rests.

But there's another, more insidious reason to avoid contact with your employees as much as possible. It's common knowledge that people who spend a significant amount of time together begin to assume similar characteristics. You've experienced it yourself if you've ever traveled to another part of the world and found your accent and intonation changing ever so slightly to mirror the people around you. And what's true of vacations is true in your working world as well.

31% of employees in one survey indicated that their supervisor gave them "the silent treatment"

Way to go, 31% of supervisors!

The best tyrants are invisible, powers that none can see and no one can approach. Because as every good tyrant knows, the more time you spend with your subordinates, the more you will become like them.

And what exactly are they like?

Time to Buy Yourself a Ten Foot Pole!

Millions of dollars have been spent on studies, surveys, and analyses designed to understand the motivation of the typical employee. So much has been written about the subject, in fact, that it can be hard to find the good information in all the noise. Fortunately for you, *Unleash Your Inner Tyrant!* will take you back to a simpler time, a time when the world made more sense, to help you better understand your employees and why you need to avoid them as much as possible.

Some of you might already be familiar with Theory X and Theory Y, management philosophies developed in the 1960s by Douglas McGregor, a professor at the MIT Sloan School of Management. Theories X and Y were essentially two opposing sets of assumptions about how employees think, operate, and are motivated.

In a nutshell, Theory X argues that employees are naturally lazy, dislike work, shun responsibility for their actions at every opportunity, and are only in it for the money. Managers with a Theory X mentality believe that the best way to motivate their congenitally defective employees is through threat, coercion, fear, and the occasional monetary incentive. A Theory X workplace is hierarchical in nature, punitive in nature, and peppered with rigid controls to prevent employees from doing damage to the company through inattention and their natural gross incompetence.

Theory Y, on the other hand, argues that employees are intrinsically motivated, enjoy working, and are skilled and creative problem solvers. These employees require little outside assistance to stay motivated and on task, and they take responsibility for their successes *and* failures. A Theory Y workplace is characterized by trust, sharing, a sense of community, and open avenues of communication.

I think it goes without saying which philosophy any aspiring tyrant should believe in.

Theory X, and Theory X alone, is the way you need to view your employees. Again, the basic highlights:

Basic Tenets of Theory X

- Employees are naturally lazy
- Employees naturally dislike work
- Employees will avoid work whenever possible
- Employees need to be controlled and threatened with punishments in order to get them to do anything

Now if you're reading this carefully, you'll realize that it will be impossible for you to remain completely separated from your employees. In order to avoid becoming lazy yourself, you'll need to stay away from your lazy employees; and yet, at the same time, you won't be able to threaten and browbeat them into submission if you're always operating from a distance. It's a delicate balancing act, and you are occasionally going to have to get your hands dirty.

But there's one other important point to understand about your employees that should bring home the importance of remaining aloof and above as often as possible. This is something Douglas McGregor overlooked in his formulation of Theory X and Theory Y, which is surprising considering that it's true of all employees regardless of the management philosophy you follow. It's probably the most important thing you can ever hope to learn about the nature of employees in general, and it could very well save your life. And here it is:

Employees spread disease

That's right, my aspiring tyrant. Employees are perhaps the single greatest vector in the transmission of disease that the world has ever known. They're like rats, crawling all over each other and infecting themselves and everything they come in contact with. Every time you put people into groups, diseases happen.

Don't believe me? Fine. It's a rather bold claim to make, I suppose.

So don't believe me, then. Believe history. Because if there's one thing I've learned in my time on Earth, it's this: dead people don't lie. They couldn't lie even if they wanted to. Because they're dead.

History Time!
Employees: Nature's Deadliest Virus

You already know that dealing with your employees is the most tedious and unpleasant part of your day. But did you know that your employees can actually kill you? Since the beginning of recorded history, employees have played a major part in almost every plague, famine, and natural disaster that has afflicted every human culture.

Consider the Black Death, a plague which swept through 14th century Europe and eventually killed approximately 30% of that continent's inhabitants. Many people have placed the blame for this plague on black rats, which carried the disease and helped it spread. But since those rats originated in Asia, they wouldn't even have gotten to Europe if it hadn't been for the employees who worked the ships and overland trade routes that connected Asian sellers to European merchants. Chinese craftsmen weren't about to walk themselves all the way to Venice and back just to sell a few bolts of silk, and Spanish nobles weren't about to walk themselves all the way to Shanghai just to buy a few pieces of porcelain. It was the employees that made it all possible. Without employees, the Black Death would never have happened.

And the same is true in a thousand other instances. The glaciers wouldn't be melting if it weren't for employees working the oil fields and building the machines that require oil for their smooth operation. The Amazon rain forests wouldn't be disappearing if it weren't for employees wielding the chainsaws and planting the palm oil trees.

So the next time you see an employee, remember that he or she is to blame for all the misery that has ever befallen our species. They are murderers. They have killed before, they will kill again, and they deserve nothing but your contempt.

If that's not enough incentive for you to keep your distance from your employees, I don't know what will be.

Congratulations are Probably in Order!

Now fortunately, many of you are probably already good at avoiding contact with your underlings. Remember that 25-year Gallup poll I mentioned earlier in this chapter? Well, turns out that through their conversations with 80,000 managers in over 400 companies they learned all kinds of things. And one of the most interesting - and heartening, at least for the purposes of *Unleash Your Inner Tyrant!* - is this particular finding:

The average total time managers spend discussing each employee's style and performance is approximately
four hours per employee per year.

That's right. Half a day a year spent talking about work with each of the people who answer to you. And that's great! That's hardly any time at all.

But that's just the average. So the next time you have a moment to yourself, try to figure out how much time you actually spend talking about work with the people who work for you – not about the work they have to do, which I'm sure you discuss all the time, but how they *do* that work and how they *feel* about how they do that work. If you're anywhere close to this 4-hour-a-year average, then congratulations! You've got the hang of this. You've already learned an important truth: that your employees are like the parts of a car.[2] You need them, but you don't need to know anything about them. You just get in and drive. You do your thing, they do their thing, and never the twain shall meet.

Until one of them breaks. And what do you do with a broken employee? Same thing you do with a broken car – get rid of it, and get yourself a new one. Easy as pie! You'll be getting rid of an annoying and potentially disease-infested subordinate, and your lack of empathy will ensure that those employees who remain loathe every moment under your supervision. That's what I call a win-win!

But What If I'm Above the 4-Hour-A-Year Average?

Relax. This wouldn't be the best management and leadership book in the history of ever if I didn't have an answer for everything. I know that you might have spent far too long in the company of your employees. I know you've made the mistake of wishing some of them "Happy Birthday" and asking about their nauseating hopes and dreams. And if so, then I'm sure you're looking for ways to scale back. There are several ways to do this:

---

[2] With diseases.

Becoming a Hermit 101

- ***Keep your office separate.*** Hiding behind a closed door is one thing (re-read *"Establish Positional Dominance"* for a refresher if you need one), but it's even better to keep your office in a separate part of the building - or better yet, in a separate building entirely! Employees can't bother you if they can't reach you.

- ***Keep irregular hours.*** You've tackled the *where*, now focus on the *when*. This technique has been perfected by college professors at every university in America. Pay attention to how effectively they avoid their students. They're masters at it. In case you're curious, that's why they call it a Master's degree.

- ***Rout all calls through voice mail.*** People will initially leave you a message and expect that you'll return the call. When you don't, though, they'll call again, but many of them won't leave a message because they won't want to seem pushy. And eventually, as long as you don't return calls, people will stop leaving messages altogether. Success!

- ***Instruct your secretary or assistant to always say you're busy.*** A popular approach of agents, producers, and others in the entertainment world, this approach is even better than the one above. After all, your employees shouldn't have access to your telephone number in the first place.

But your best friend in this endeavor, the one that will help you remain aloof and above better than any other technique in the tyrant's toolbox, is…

The Self-Appraisal!

If you are not already forcing your employees to conduct regular self-appraisals, you need to start immediately. Just as your org chart is the most effective tool to help you establish positional dominance, the self-appraisal is unquestionably your best weapon in the fight to remain separate from the people who work for you.

Why? For several reasons. First, the self-appraisal allows you to eliminate the hassle of doing any actual work; all you have to do is pass out a paper or send out an email, and your job is done. Second, the self-appraisal by its very nature ensures that you will not spend any time or energy doing any critical thinking whatsoever about your workforce. It will virtually ensure that you remain well beneath the 4-hour-a-year average that you should be shooting for. Third, everyone on the planet *hates* filling out self-appraisals, which of course is why you should use them. This line of thinking really fits more into the *Trample Your Underlings…Then Trample Them Again!* section, but consider this a taste of what's to come.

But finally, and most importantly, the self-appraisal forces your employees to try and figure out how to best articulate their usefulness to you and your company without sounding too impressive. None of your employees are going to give themselves failing grades, of course – who'd commit that kind of career suicide? – which effectively negates most of the 'thoughtful self-analysis' rationale behind issuing a self-appraisal in the first place. But they also know that the best grade they can put on their own self-appraisal is a B. They can't say they're *too* good, or then they'll look arrogant, self-serving, and not reflective enough. And since the best grade they can hope for is a B, the act of filling out a self-appraisal makes it almost impossible for your employees, no matter how good they actually are, to ever argue for a raise. It is a masterful invention - time-consuming, frustrating, and of almost no value to anyone involved.

So there you have it. You have effectively isolated yourself from the people who do the work that keeps your company in business. Congratulations.

But you can't afford to relax yet. There is one potentially disastrous consequence of remaining aloof and above. Yes, it will keep you away from those worthless, pestilential people you're obliged to keep on the payroll; but it will also keep you away from any of your employees who might be plotting your overthrow. A successful tyrant must always be aware of the fact that tyranny is extremely difficult to maintain. A quick glance through the history books offers several disturbing examples of tyrants who fell from grace precisely because they failed to stop threats to their power in time. Don't mistake me: I don't want you to spend any more time with your employees than is absolutely necessary. But if you're not careful, you won't discover any rebellions until it's too late to stop them.

So, how do you prevent your employees from mounting a successful insurrection? How can you prevent them from threatening your hegemony? The answers are coming. Turn the page.

Bureaucracy and Other Ways to Stifle Communication!

"Bureaucracy is the art
of making the possible impossible."
Javier Pascual Salcedo

"I bought a donut and they gave me a receipt for the donut...I can't imagine a scenario where I would have to prove that I bought a donut. To some skeptical friend, 'Don't even act like I didn't get that donut, I've got the documentation right here...'"
Mitch Hedberg

"Bureaucracies are inherently antidemocratic. Bureaucrats derive their power from their position in the structure, not from their relations with the people they are supposed to serve. The people are not masters of the bureaucracy, but its clients."
Alan Keyes

You really should have seen this coming, and not only because the table of contents told you it was coming. One of the most important objectives of a successful tyrant is to obfuscate the channels of communication. Bureaucracy, people - *that* is what we're shooting for. The more approvals every action requires, the more steps you can create between the beginning and end of every process, and the more involved you can be in decisions that you have no business being involved in, the more effective your tyranny will be.

Most people say that good communication should be a two-way street. But effective tyrants follow a different kind of city planning. For them, communication is like driving in Washington, D.C. Have you ever tried to drive in that city? It's enough to make you want to drive your car straight into the Potomac. I don't think there's a more perfect visual representation of the power of bureaucracy than the streets of our nation's capital. Right angles? That's crazy talk. Oh, and I have an idea – let's let everybody turn left wherever they want *without creating any left-turn lanes!!!!* That won't bring traffic to an almost perpetual halt, will it? Freaking genius, I tell you.

The point, my aspiring tyrant, is that redundancy, confusion, and misdirection are the order of the day. A successful tyrant must always be aware of the fact that most dictatorships eventually fail. Instead of passing the baton to their chosen successors, many tyrants end up overthrown by the very forces they have spent so long attempting to repress. And the best way to avoid that fate is to keep those beneath you separate from one another, so that they never have the opportunity to work effectively together, share ideas, or really do anything to threaten your hegemony. You don't trust your kids to drive the nice car, why would you trust your childlike employees to handle the important accounts?

The Myths

Now again, the enemies of tyranny have been busy, propagating myths and lies designed to make you uncomfortable with the notion of embarking on your own bureaucratic journey. Perhaps you've heard their vicious slander and baseless hypotheses. Perhaps you've even been persuaded to work toward a collaborative model of information-sharing, to keep the lines of communication open and streamlined.

And if you have, do yourself a favor. Put this book down. Take a deep breath. Then, punch yourself in the face as hard as you can. Allow the pain of it to clear your mind, then pick this book back up when you're ready to hear reason.

Let me show you how you need to proceed. I'm going to share with you the results of a few studies:

- In *Controlling the Costs of Conflict*, Karl Slaikeu and Ralph Hasson offer several examples of the benefits of collaborative communication. Specifically, Brown and Root reported an 80% reduction in outside litigation expenses by introducing a systemic approach to collaboration and conflict resolution; Motorola reported a 75% reduction over 6 years; National Cash Register Corporation reported a drop in pending lawsuits from 263 to 28 between 1984 and 1993; the U.S. Air Force reported that by taking a collaborative approach to conflict management in a construction project, it completed the project 144 days ahead of schedule and $12 million under budget.

- In the 1970s, Reg Revans, a professor of industrial management at the University of Manchester, resigned his post to work in

> Belgium to help improve that country's industrial output. Working with five universities and 23 large businesses, Revans put Action Learning into practice, which he describes thusly: "I wasn't there to teach anyone anything. We got people talking to each other, asking questions. People from the airline business talked to people from chemical companies. People shared knowledge and experience." The result of all this free and open communication? The Belgian economy enjoyed a spectacular renaissance – during the 1970s Belgian industrial productivity rose 102%, compared with 28% in the U.K. and also above the growth rates of the United States, Germany, and Japan. In fact, in 2000 Belgium was 1st in the world in GDP per person per hour. Revans was subsequently awarded the nation's top civilian honor by the King of Belgium.

Seems compelling, doesn't it? And it is. Which is exactly why I'm going to ignore those studies.

Why? Because I'm a *tryant!* Tyrants are not beholden to the whims of research. They don't base their actions on empirical evidence, or the half-baked theories of academics. They don't consult others about the best ways to maximize everyone's productivity and effectiveness. In fact, they don't listen to *anybody* – haven't I made that clear enough by now?

Besides, who in the history of ever has said, "When I grow up, I want to be model myself on the practices of the Belgian people." Nobody, that's who. Aside from that syrup container they call a Belgian waffle and a handful of delicious beers and chocolates, that country has given the world absolutely nothing of value.[1]

So what's it going to be? Are you going to model yourself after a people who own more bicycles than cars, or are you going to create a maddeningly complicated working environment? The choice should be obvious.

The Basics

So, how does one become a world-class bureaucrat? Any number of ways – there are 4,000,002 ways, in fact. Below is a sampling of some of my favorites. And while all of the following techniques are sufficient in and of themselves, the best of you will find a way to use all of them.

- ***Create unnecessary redundancies*** I'm sure you've all seen *Office Space* and remember fondly the opening scene with the endless conversations about TPS reports. If not, run out to your nearest Blockbuster[2] and rent yourself a copy. And if your nearest Blockbuster is out of copies,[3] just schedule a meeting whose purpose is to determine when your team should have its next meeting. That should be easy enough.

---

[1] "Wait a second! You forgot lace. Belgian lace is considered some of the best in the – " Shut up.

[2] Ha! Run out to your nearest Blockbuster – oh, I crack me *up*! Does anybody do that anymore? More on Blockbuster's successful self-destruction in an upcoming chapter.

[3] Ha again! Man, I am on a roll today!

- ***Withhold information*** A classic tyrant tactic. There are several advantages to this approach. For one, it's a great way to get rumors started. The more gaps you create in your subordinates' understanding of the big picture, the more they'll attempt to fill those gaps with whatever they think they know. And most of the time they're wrong – because if you'll remember from earlier, your employees are idiots – which is what makes rumors so much fun! But also, the more information you withhold, the more your subordinates will be forced to rely on you to fill them in, since you'll be the only one who knows everything. Withholding information is a great way to solidify your power – and if you're able to do it while still remaining aloof and above when your employees absolutely require whatever information you're withholding…well, how much better can it get?

- ***Act and speak inconsistently*** This one is my personal favorite. You ever watch four-year-olds try to talk their way out of getting punished for misbehaving? They can never keep their stories straight! Seriously, rent your neighbor's children for an afternoon[4] and watch them in action.

---

[4] I've never understood why parents pay babysitters to watch their kids, when you could just rent them to people who are considering parenthood for themselves. You make a little money, they get some valuable parenting experience – everybody wins! Seriously, I think it's a great idea, and now that I've shared it with you, I know you're going to consider it.

They'll teach you what you might have forgotten: logic has no place in bureaucracy. So if somebody offers to help you, berate them for insinuating that you don't know what you're doing, then find somebody else and ask for the same help the other person was offering. Write long-winded emails and incomprehensibly brief reports; give two different answers to the same question, or the same answer to two different questions; wear brown shoes with black pants; eat at your desk and return phone calls in the bathroom. Eventually you'll be so confused about what you're supposed to be doing that you won't know how to get back to center even if you make the mistake of wanting to.

- ***Agree (or disagree) with everything*** Doesn't matter which way you go here, the end result will be the same.

- ***Say the same thing multiple times*** Boy, do I love this one! Make sure you change your language just enough so that everyone realizes that all you did was reword somebody else's report or email.

I'd thought about ending this section by simply restating, in slightly different language, everything I've just told you, but I decided not to. Because if there's anything that frustrates people, it's hearing the same thing twice. Isn't that right? I know it's right. Because if there's anything that frustrates people, it's hearing the same thing twice.

I could keep going, you know.

Bureaucracy in Practice

Want to see the above techniques put into practice? Well, look no further! As with many things, the art of bureaucracy is best explained through example. And fortunately, an overwhelming number of attendees at my keynote presentations were more than happy to share stories of the bureaucrats and communication-killers in their professional lives. I've included a couple of my favorites. With any luck, you'll see a little bit of yourself reflected in them!

Storytime!

Glen R. is a CEO in the healthcare industry. Among his various duties, he is contractually obligated to work with a small governmental agency to provide various services – an agency whose CEO is among the world's best bureaucrats.

"He is the most frustrating, confounding, exasperating 'manager' I have encountered in my 40+ years in healthcare," Glen says. "Here are a few of his approaches to relationships and management that create havoc and uncertainty in any and all interactions with this agency."

Are you rubbing your hands with glee? I sure am!

"The man is a master of revisionist planning. I have sat through multiple long, tedious, and contentious meetings where we eventually decide upon an agreed plan of action and approach to resolving issues. We shake hands and leave and

I'm thinking we finally are making headway. Wrong! As soon as he leaves the face-to-face, his mind is at work 'interpreting' what was agreed to or otherwise devising strategies to completely ignore or revise the plans. When we get back together to update the status of the plan, one of two things will have occurred: when he puts his version of the agreement into action or on paper, it takes an entirely different direction, tone or flavor until it does not even resemble what was agreed to; or he decides to completely ignore what was agreed upon and no action is ever taken. He runs out of time, staffing changes have occurred – there's always something, and he always has a justification for his non-action. The problem will come up again, of course, and he'll just agree to do it again and ignore it again. I cannot tell you how many times this has happened."

Great! Well, it looks like we've got redundancies, inconsistent actions, and blanket agreements all covered. Can we do anything about withholding information?

"Absolutely," Glen says. "We're all familiar with the 'mushroom theory' of management. Its major tenets include keeping people in the dark with no contact with the outside world, and then constantly covering them in manure. This individual is a master at putting this theory into practice. Through extensive and manipulative efforts he keeps all potential communications between constituents from happening. He facilitates extensive separation of communication and NEVER[5] allows those with similar interests

[5] The all caps here are Glen's, not mine. He wanted everybody to know that he was shouting while he said this, and if you can do him the favor of imagining a little foam forming at the corners of his mouth at this point, he'd appreciate it.

but separate opinions to actually sit down and discuss the issues. Naturally, because he never lets people discuss important issues, nothing gets resolved. It creates this perpetual climate of turmoil and uncertainty that he sees as a security blanket because he is the only one with access to all information, and he can control what is shared with whom and when it is done."

Kudos to you, anonymous government tyrant! You've done your part to help cement the idea that government is the ultimate bureaucracy. I'm certain that the only thing keeping any of your employees around for more than a year is the stability of government-job benefits – which I'm sure you'd take away if you could![6]

Advanced Techniques

Already doing all of the above? Then try these approaches on for size:

- ***Auto-response EVERYTHING*** Nobody should be able to send you a direct email. Nobody should be able to leave you a direct message. Everything, everything, *everything* should be routed through at least one roadblock. Your auto-reply should *always* be on, and the best of you will indicate that you'll respond to each

[6] I wrote this sentence a couple months before half the states in America proposed legislation to curtail and in some cases eliminate government-job benefits. Man, am I psychic or what?

person in the order that their email was received. The Internet thought it could streamline communications, did it? Well, two can play at that game.

- ***Automated menus!!!*** The bane of every caller's existence, which is why you need to install one for yourself. There is literally no one alive that enjoys being trapped in the endless purgatory of Automated Menu-Land. Which is why all of us curse like sailors until we're connected to an actual living human being. The more that unflappably polite lady keeps saying, "Sorry, I didn't understand you," the more I wish she was a real person so I could choke the life out of her.

- ***Poorly designed websites!*** Dear God, there are a ton of these. My favorites are the ones that don't let you hit the 'back' key to return to the previous page. My second favorites are the ones that open a new window *every* time you hit a link. The bronze medal goes to websites that have hot buttons scattered all around the page with no discernable order. And the participation ribbon goes to websites that offer a single page of endlessly scrolling text – you know, the kind that remind you of those dot-matrix printers with their endless scrolling roll of dot-matrix paper. Ease of use is for winners, and the people you're attempting to oppress should never, under any circumstances, feel like winners.

The Results

So, where will all this lead? What can establishing an effective bureaucracy accomplish for you?

I think a few statistics are in order.

**According to one study,
92% of senior executives and managers say
they communicate well with their subordinates.
However, only 59% of executives and managers say
that their supervisors communicate well.**

**According to another study, 73% of executives
believe they communicate well or very well with their
subordinates. However, only 35% of managers felt that
their superiors communicated well with them.**

**According to yet another study....nah, nevermind.
I think you get the point!**

This is the legacy that bureaucracy can bring you. The more effective your bureaucracy is, the larger the disconnect you'll create between your perception of reality and your subordinates' perceptions. The more difficult it is for people to communicate information, the more gaps in knowledge you'll help create. Those gaps will cause different people to believe different things, to operate on different assumptions, and to attempt problem-solving with different and often incompatible approaches. Extended out on a long enough timeline, these misperceptions can create an utterly impossible working environment - impossible, that is, without your direct supervision. If you are the *only* one with all the relevant information, if you are the *only* one that people can come to for answers, then you will also be the *only* indispensable member of your team. Will everybody hate you? Of course they will, because they'll know that things could be running so much more smoothly and efficiently. But who cares? You're not trying to be friends with them. Why would you? They're *diseased*, remember?

But there's another reason you should strive to create an unnecessarily complicated system of checks and balances. And that something happens to be hiding just around the corner.

Page-turning time!!!

Trust No One!

"Ideas are more powerful than guns.
We would not let our enemies have guns,
why should we let them have ideas?"
Joseph Stalin

I feel like shaking things up a bit, so we're going to begin this chapter with a fable. You might have heard it before.

Once upon a time there was a scorpion that wanted to cross a river. His side of the river was in a low-performing school district, you see, and the other side of the river also had all the best restaurants and a lower corporate tax rate. So he began to research the rudiments of shipbuilding and was about to acquire the necessary woodworking tools and look for a handful of reputable contractors when he saw a frog nearby.

"Excuse me, frog," the scorpion said. "Are you going across the river?"

"Yes," said the frog.

"Well, what a happy coincidence for the purposes of this fable! I feel like fate has brought us together, for I would also like to cross this river. Can I ride on your back while you cross?"

"I don't know," the frog said. "I'm afraid that you will sting me if I let you close."

"Nonsense," the scorpion said. "You're such a sad, paranoid little frog. If I sting you, you'll drown. And if you drown, so will I. That would be bad for both of us."

Persuaded, the frog agreed. The scorpion hopped on his little froggy back, and together the two of them made their way across the river.

Then, just as they made it to the far side, the scorpion stung the frog. As the frog was sinking, he asked the scorpion, "Why did you do this? After I helped you, why would you turn on me?"

The scorpion shrugged his scorpion shoulders. "I'm a scorpion. It's my nature to sting. That's what I do. I didn't mean to, honestly – it just happened."

The frog was angry, but not for long, because he was also paralyzed. Soon he sank to the bottom of the river and drowned, and his anger drowned with him. He tried to curse the scorpion – "Traitor! Murderer! Villain! I curse you and your family!" the frog tried to say – but the words didn't come out right because he was drowning, and so the curse didn't work.

What's the moral of this story? It's pretty simple. If you trust people, you'll end up dead at the bottom of a river.

Let me make myself perfectly clear. When it comes to being a great tyrant, trust is the great destroyer. The second you allow yourself to trust your subordinates, bad things are going to happen. Healthy marriages might be built on trust; you might have to succumb to the dangers of trust if you're planning an expedition to scale the Himalayas. And you should probably trust the pilot of your airplane to do his or her job well, or else you're going to have an awfully uncomfortable and sweaty-palmed flight. But when it comes to establishing an effective and enduring tyranny, trust is a luxury you cannot afford.

But don't take my word for it. History is replete with examples of people and organizations that allowed themselves to be blinded by trust, with devastating results:

Still Feel Like Trusting People?

- In 44 B.C., Julius Caesar installed himself as dictator of the Roman Empire. He was able to do this because he had a massive army backing him up, which is something every serious tyrant should really consider trying to get. However, he also had friends, which is something every serious tyrant should really consider trying to get rid of. One of his friends was a man named Lucius Brutus. Caesar trusted Brutus, and Brutus used that trust to stab Caesar in the back. And the front, and the sides, and pretty much everywhere else. Some friend.

- In 1976, Steve Jobs founded Apple Computers along with his friend Steve Wozniak. In 1983 Jobs hired former Pepsi-Cola president John Sculley to help run Apple. And in 1984, Steve Wozniak and John Sculley repaid Steve Jobs for all his hard work by forcing him out of the very company he founded.

- In 2002, WorldCom was humming along, engaged in highly successful and completely undetected accounting fraud. Then their Vice President of Internal Audit, Cynthia Cooper, came along and ruined everything by letting the whole world know that WorldCom was overvalued by around $4 billion. Thanks a lot, Cynthia.

- In 1995, I made the mistake of telling a good friend of mine that I was planning to ask a certain girl to Homecoming. Then he went and asked her himself. Jerk. Guess who's not going to be accepting *your* friend request on Facebook? That'd be me.

I think I've made my point.

Overcoming the Trusting Trend

Now I know that this might be difficult for you. You've read too many business books with their nauseating focus on the positive power of trust, and they have brainwashed you. I warned you about this when we began the book, but the pervasiveness of the idea that trust is a good thing might seem to indicate that all those authors know what they're talking about. But the real truth is this: if you tell a lie long enough, people will eventually believe it.

Some of the more audacious lies I've come across include:

- Economist John Helliwell found that trust is the greatest contributor to workplace happiness, beating out pay, workload, or perks. According to his research, a one-point increase on the trust scale is equivalent to the psychological benefits associated with a 40% wage increase.

- Trust functions as a positive feedback loop. If managers trust their employees, employees will repay their managers by returning that trust, which managers repay in turn by trusting their employees even more.

- The more trust that exists in the workplace, the higher the productivity. There are also numerous studies that correlate high levels of trust with reduced employee turnover, lower employee absenteeism, and higher levels of customer satisfaction.

- The Container Store, which in 2009 made Fortune Magazine's "100 Best Companies to Work For" for the 9th year in a row, works so hard to create a culture of trust that the company makes its financial statements available to everyone in the company.

- In a 2002 Harvard Business Review article titled "The high cost of lost trust," Tony Simons surveyed 6,500 Holiday Inn employees at 76 international hotel sites and found that those

> hotels whose managers did what they said they would do – in other words, managers who earned their employees' trust – were more profitable than their less trustworthy counterparts. In fact, on a 5-point scale of trust and integrity, each one-eighth-point improvement resulted in a 2.5% increase in hotel revenues.

Do not allow yourself to succumb to this poisonous way of thought. We've already discussed the dangers of doing anything that the so-called "Best Companies to Work For" would do. And what exactly is this magical 'trust scale' that John Helliwell speaks of? Sounds fake to me.

But allow me to offer perhaps the most powerful example of the problems that trusting your employees can lead to. There's a famous quote about trust by noted teddy bear enthusiast Theodore Roosevelt, a quote that has been paraphrased or outright plagiarized in just about every business book written in the last 50 years. I'm sure you're familiar with it:

"The best executive is the one who has sense enough to pick good people to do what he wants done, and self-restraint enough to keep from meddling with them while they do it."

Obviously, Teddy trusted the people who worked for him. He relied on their counsel, listened to their opinions, and thoughtfully considered their advice. He believed that he was incapable of doing everything alone, and so he turned to trust as a strategy for success.

And look where it got him. You might be tempted to focus on his enduring legacy in establishing our first national parks. You might zero in on the fact that most historians agree that Theodore Roosevelt was one of our five greatest presidents, right up there with Abraham Lincoln and Millard Fillmore. But 'Best Of' lists are notoriously unreliable and easy to manipulate; after all, how else would James Joyce's Ulysses, a book that exactly 13 people have ever read and that absolutely nobody understands, be praised as one of the greatest novels of all time? No, the rosy mirror of considered, historical consensus is not a good guide.

But physical monuments are. Opinions can change, but stone doesn't lie. And there is absolutely no denying that Theodore Roosevelt got the crappiest spot on Mount Rushmore.

Look at him, hiding there in the mountain's divot, shoved to the back of the family portrait. Most people don't even remember that that's him. Is that how you want to be remembered? Do you want to be the giant stone head next to all those other more famous giant stone heads?

I don't think so. It's first place or no place, baby.

Getting Down to Business

So, how can you let everybody know how little you trust them? The key is to let your employees *know* that you don't trust them. They need to be aware of the fact that you do not think them capable of making intelligent decisions. Remember Theory X? Time to put that philosophy into practice.

Profiles in Tyranny: Henry Ford

Founder of Ford Motors, Henry Ford was one of the richest men in the history of the world, worth an estimated $188 billion in 2010 dollars. If he were alive today, he'd probably buy Michigan, turn it into a private kingdom, secede from America, and use it as a base of operations from which he would eventually conquer Earth. There is no question that Henry Ford knew how to run a successful business. And there is also no question that he did not trust his workforce to do the right thing – the right thing, of course, being whatever Henry Ford said it was.

Case in point: in 1914 Ford instituted the $5 workday, which at the time was twice the going rate for unskilled factory workers. The policy stands today as one of his most insightful business ideas. In one stroke, Ford's $5-a-day policy reduced employee turnover from over 200% to nearly zero, which ultimately saved the company money in reduced training and hiring costs. It also caused an influx of skilled mechanics, engineers, and other auto workers to Detroit in order to take advantage of Ford's generosity, which helped Detroit become America's auto manufacturing hub. And it ensured that Ford's workers were making enough money to purchase the products they were producing. All around, it was a brilliant example of the power of paying better-than-average wages.

But Ford's generosity came with a cost. In order to qualify for the $5-a-day wage, Ford employees were required to pass an inspection by Ford's Social Department, a group of approximately 50 investigators who were tasked with ensuring that employees lived in a manner in keeping with Ford's idea of propriety. Employees who drank, kept late hours, or engaged in 'loose morality' – a conveniently abstract term that could mean whatever Ford wanted it to mean – were denied entry into Ford Motor's generous wage system. Think of it like an early version of the House Un-American Activities Commission – and we all know how fantastically that worked out.

Enough said.

Was Ford right to hold his employees to his own standards of morality? Absolutely. It's a proven fact that people who occasionally drink and stay out late are incapable of having good ideas or offering anything valuable to the world. I can't seem to find the source of that proven fact, but trust me – it's true.

Profiles in Tyranny: Harry Cohn

Do you remember back in *Establish Positional Dominance* when we discussed Harry Cohn's practice of installing hidden microphones everywhere, listening in on his workers' conversations and shouting at them over loudspeakers if he heard something he didn't like?

Good. Just wanted to make sure.

At this point, I imagine some of you might be a bit disconcerted. Perhaps you're not currently in a position to control wages – or more importantly, to attach privacy and morality restrictions to those wage increases. Perhaps you don't have the budget to install hidden surveillance equipment in the offices of all your officemates. And perhaps you're worried that, in an age of cell phones and instant messaging, the sight of you installing loudspeakers all around the office will make you look like a giant dork.

Fear not. Ford and Cohn are men of another time. They should serve as role models, not necessarily models of behavior. Their legacy can still live on in the several simple, inexpensive ways that you can illustrate your lack of trust in today's modern workplace.

Treating Your Employees Like the Parasites They Are!

- ***Monitoring lunch hours*** Just because your employees have graduated from high school doesn't mean that you should treat them any differently than you'd treat a 10th-grader.

- ***Ringing a bell to signal the end of a shift or workday*** Some companies actually do this. Seriously. I had trouble believing it myself. But man, what a great idea! If you do this long enough, eventually you can make your employees salivate whenever you want them to. I don't know why you'd want to make them salivate on cue, but it's an option. Thanks, Pavlov!

- ***Not allowing your employees access to necessary equipment*** There are several ways to implement this approach, the most common of which is to require employees to undergo a multi-step process in order to check out equipment they need on a regular basis in order to do the job they were hired to do. For maximum achievement, the successful tyrant will accompany this policy with frequent complaints about how slowly his or her employees are working. This dual-pronged attack has been known to cause some employees to self-destruct in the middle of very public places, which is always fun to watch.

- ***Editing and correcting all of your subordinates' work*** No matter how minor or routine, you need to make sure you have a say in the final product, because there is simply no way that your employees are capable of handling any assignment on their own. The best of you will make 'changes' to your employees' work that don't actually change anything (for example, changing "We need to implement this strategy before December 31st" to "We need to put this strategy into practice by year end.")

- ***Requiring all employees to carry see-through bags and purses*** You never know what those thieves are going to take from you.

- ***Institute a convoluted and difficult return policy*** Your lack of trust should not be limited to your employees. Your customers cannot be trusted, either. The only reason they would ever choose to return a product - the *only* reason - is because they are trying to make your life more difficult. Do not allow them to rule you in such fashion. Refuse their returns, remind them that they're adults who made a decision about buying something, and tell them that responsible people live with the decisions they make. And if that doesn't work, call the police.

According to one survey of 13,000 workers,
fewer than 40% of employees
expressed trust and confidence in their senior leaders.

If all of these methods of demonstrating your lack of trust in your employees are not enough for you, get into the habit of standing over them while they're working. Lean it a bit, leer at them, watch them over their shoulder, maybe sift through their trash when they're not around – or better yet, when they are! If possible, provide yourself with a glass-walled office so that you can monitor your employees without having to leave your desk. Stand with your arms folded, and glare at them for at least ninety minutes a day. If you have an open office plan, invest in a telescope and train it on the desks of your workers. Make sure it's pointing in a slightly different position every morning so that your employees know you're actually using it.

And for those of you who would like to maintain a thin veneer of secrecy, do not underestimate the power of the periscope.

How You Will Know If You've Succeeded

There are several ways to confirm whether or not your lack of trust in your employees is having the desired effect. The nice thing about trust, or its lack, is that it is almost always reciprocated. If you trust others, they will trust you. If you do not trust others, they will not trust you. But here's the really important point:

If you're *the boss* and do not trust others, eventually your employees will mistrust *themselves*.

That's right! A healthy dose of mistrust on your end can infect your entire workplace like a virus, poisoning the minds and self-perceptions of everyone around you. After all, what kind of person would be so openly mistrustful of those around him or her unless there were a good reason to be?

(The answer is 'A tyrant would!' but your employees won't necessarily know that.)

And so, you'll know that you've built a healthy culture of mistrust when your employees never offer their own opinions and always agree with everything you say, because they don't trust themselves to have intelligent thoughts of their own. You'll know you've done well when your employees bring you items for approval that you *both* know should not require your direct attention, because they don't trust themselves to handle even the smallest assignments without your input. You'll know you've built an appropriately toxic culture when you cannot remember the last time one of your employees offered a productive or insightful thought at a team meeting, because they do not trust themselves to have ideas you'll be interested in – nor should they!

But you'll know you've gone just about as far as it is possible to go if anybody ever starts to compare you to Rupert Murdoch.

Profiles in Tyranny: Rupert Murdoch

You all know who Rupert Murdoch is. He turned his father's modest publishing business into one of the largest media empires in the world. He has significant interests in all things media – newspapers, television stations, Internet concerns, etc. He renounced his Australian citizenship and became an American citizen so that he could own media companies in the United States. And he is rumored to be currently trying to purchase the Moon so that he can turn it into a private getaway for Republicans in case the Democrats ever conquer Earth[1].

But do you know the methods by which his fortune has been acquired? Why, it's a veritable smorgasbord of tyrannies. There's the 2009 revelation that *News of the World* engaged in systematic phone hacking of random politicians, celebrities, and other notables in a blind attempt to find compromising information to report about. There's collusion with the British government under Margaret Thatcher to destroy the power of the print unions. There's a host of lawsuits regarding anti-competitive business practices, although none of them have stuck – and thank God they haven't, or else we might not have the luxury of Glenn Beck's fair and balanced reporting.[2]

But when it comes to trust, Rupert Murdoch is known the world over as one of Earth's most notoriously untrusting CEOs. In fact Andrew Neil, former editor for the *Sunday Times* and one of Murdoch's closest aides for 11 years, says of his former boss: "He travels alone, but then he is a loner. The only people who are really close to him are his wife, his children, his sister, and his mother. He has no real friends. He does not allow himself to become intimate with anybody else, for he never knows when he will have to turn on them."

Music to my ears, people.

---

[1] Which of course wouldn't be a possibility if Henry Ford were alive, since he'd have already conquered it.

[2] It has come to my attention that Glenn Beck is no longer selling gold and freeze-died apocalypse rations on Fox News anymore. That, people, is a huge bummer. Those apocalypse rations were delicious, and now I just don't know where to get them.

Oh, and a fun fact: after Murdoch heard what Neil said about him, he had Neil deported![3]

So remember, my aspiring tyrant: every employee is your potential replacement, and friends are enemies in disguise. Now if you'll excuse me, I have to go put the finishing touches on my underground bunker.

So, where is all of this leading?

I was delivering a speech to a few hundred managers in Las Vegas, providing them with everything I've told you so far about how to create an environment of fear, self-interest, and mistrust. They were absorbing it nicely, even laughing at several parts, and very few of them were playing with their phones.[4] Afterwards, several attendees asked if there were a simple way to remember all this, an easy takeaway they could have to make sure they never made the same mistakes these tyrants did. I told them they had completely missed the purpose of the presentation.

---

[3] OK, that's not true. But it's not entirely outside the realm of possibility, which is yet another reason why Murdoch rocks as a tyrant.

[4] It seems to have become a common practice for people to check their phones almost constantly while they sit in meetings and presentations. I will admit, it's even happened to me, even though I deliver perhaps the most awesome presentations you'll ever see short of a heavy metal concert or a Bill Cosby show. And I swear, the next time somebody pulls out their phone while I'm giving a talk or leading a meeting, I'm going to jump off the stage, grab it from their surprised fingers, and smash their phone against the floor. It'll cost me about $200 and one seriously irritated conference attendee, but it'll ensure that nobody ever pulls their phone out while I'm talking again. Just a thought, managers.

But then I realized that there *is* an easy takeaway, a single concept so perfect for its ability to tyrannize that I couldn't believe I hadn't thought of it myself. One beautiful word that summarizes everything I've attempted to teach you so far. And I'll bet you already know what that word is.

Micromanagement!

"The universities are available only to those
who share my revolutionary beliefs."
Fidel Castro

"If I had enough arms and legs and time,
I'd do it all myself."
Harold Geneen

Here it is, my aspiring tyrant, the culmination of everything I've attempted to teach you so far – micromanagement. You know the phrase: if you want a job done right, ***do it yourself!!!!*** Your employees are incompetent nitwits, barely worth the air they breathe and *certainly* not worth the salary you pay them to do such shoddy work. They're like puppets, and you the master puppeteer. You need to be pulling all the strings all the time.

Micromanagement is the heart of creating an environment of fear, self-interest, and mistrust; it is the natural extension of everything we've talked about so far. Because *if* you are a stickler for positional authority, *if* you have no real contact with your employees, *if* you've created an unnecessarily complicated method of communicating information back and forth between the members of your workforce, and *if* you don't trust any of your employees with even the smallest amount of autonomy, then you will naturally tend toward micromanagement.

89% of employees consider 'personal autonomy and authority' to be important both professionally and psychologically

Does that statistic make you queasy? It should. Because if your employees *get* that personal autonomy and authority they so desperately crave, what does that mean to you? Since I'm a practicing micromanager, I'll tell you what it means. It means that every one of them will start to get airs. They'll make their own decisions, which will lead to them feeling important, which will lead to your employees - brace yourself - *offering ideas and suggestions of their own.* They'll be *engaged*, which is a direct threat to the tyranny you're working so hard to build.

But words are cheap. Examples say all. Here you go.

Profiles in Idiocy: Michael Abrashoff

Perhaps you've heard of Michael Abrashoff, a former Navy commander and captain of the *USS Benfold.* You would think that a man trained by the U.S. military, an organization often associated with micromanagement, rigid adherence to protocol, and an unfailing deference to authority would have learned something in his time there. But apparently he didn't.

His first mistake? Getting to know his crew. I think we've covered pretty thoroughly the advantages of remaining aloof and above, but unfortunately for Abrashoff, this book wasn't written when he was captain of the *Benfold*. And so, without me to guide him, he made the mistake of interviewing five crewpeople each day until he knew them all. The end result?

"I came to respect my people as I never had before," Abrashoff said. "Before, I never knew them, never cared about them, just assumed they were out to screw me over, and I thought I had to micromanage them. But after I got to know them, I came to respect them and then wanted to help them achieve their goals."

I know that was difficult to read. But there's more, my aspiring tyrant. Abrashoff's crimes don't end there. What I'm about to share with you is so shocking, so grotesque, that it should constitute treason.

"When I took command of the *Benfold*," Abrashoff continued, "I realized that no one, including me, is capable of making every decision. I would have to train people to think and make judgments on their own. Whenever the consequences of a decision had the potential to kill or injure someone, waste taxpayers' money, or damage the ship, I had to be consulted. Short of those contingencies, the crew was authorized to make their own decisions. Even if the decisions were wrong, I would stand by my crew. Hopefully, they would learn from their mistakes. And the more responsibility they were given, the more they learned."

Unbelievable, isn't it? Can one even be said to be 'in command' of something when that person gives his command away? In fact, Abrashoff had the audacity to write a leadership book called *It's Our Ship*. Did you hear that? "*Our*" ship. Ours. Like, yours and mine. Everybody's. It's enough to make you cry, isn't it?

> **All I can say is, thank God this man is retired. There's no telling what kind of danger our country would be in if people like Michael Abrashoff were in a position to use their 'we're all in this together' philosophy to shape American policy.**

And what exactly happened as a result of Abrashoff's embrace of servant leadership? Well, on average, fewer than 30% of sailors re-enlist after their first tour. On the *Benfold*, however, under Abrashoff's command, *100%* of career sailors signed on for another tour, a retention rate which saved the U.S. military $1.6 million in personnel-related costs in 1998.

Now, there's no denying that saving almost two million dollars is a positive outcome; after all, that's almost two million additional dollars that you'll be able to siphon into a personal account right before your retirement or ouster.[1] But look at that other statistic. 100% retention rate. 100% of his sailors stayed on, every one of them empowered to make his or her own decisions. 100% of them flush with a sense of accomplishment and purpose. Which means 100% of them are potential threats to his ultimate authority. *That's* why you have to micromanage, my aspiring tyrant, to prevent any of your underlings from ever developing the skills they'd need in order to throw you over. You know the old adage:

Teach a man to fish, and he'll be self-sufficient.
But *give* a man a fish,
and he'll be dependent on you forever.

---

[1] More on this and other exit strategies in the upcoming chapter, *Create and Escape Plan for You and Nobody Else*.

That is the true genius of micromanagement. The best micromanagers crush every independent thought out of their employee's tiny little micromanaged heads. They nit and pick and poke and prod and question and review and revise until their employees learn to stop thinking for themselves, wait for orders, and do only as they are told. If you want to be a star micromanager, then you need to work tirelessly to create a system that cannot function without your constant input.

Profiles in Tyranny: UBS

UBS is a giant Swiss financial services company – the second largest manager of private assets, in fact, with something above $2 trillion under their management. They're best known for helping thousands of Americans evade taxes by hiding billions of dollars in Swiss tax shelters, a practice which ultimately ended in a 2009 lawsuit that required UBS to pay $780 million in punitive damages to the U.S. government for conspiring to defraud the United States. They're really good with money.

And how did they become so good at helping people avoid paying their taxes? By telling their employees how to do literally everything – including dress themselves!

In late 2010, UBS published a 44-page dress code policy for its employees. No, I didn't mistype that. 44 pages. That's how many pages they felt were necessary to tell people how to dress. 44. Chances are this handbook (or handsbook, since you'd probably need two hands to hold it) was written by a team of people over several months.

What did this monstrosity of a dress code cover? Everything from what to eat (no garlic or onions) to how often men should get a haircut (once a month) to – and I'm seriously not making this up – what color underwear UBS employees are supposed to wear. (Unfortunately for all of us, the answer is skin-colored.) I'm not exactly certain who was in charge of checking to ensure that all of UBS's 64,000 employees were abstaining from wearing lacy red bras or leopard-spotted man thongs, but I can say that it's a job that would probably be very easy to get. Not a lot of applicants, I'm guessing.

Want to see some excerpts from their handbook? I know you do. It doesn't get any better than this, people:

- "You can extend the life of your knee socks and stockings by keeping your toenails trimmed and filed. Always have a spare pair. Stockings can be provisionally repaired with transparent nail polish and a bit of luck."

- "Glasses should always be kept clean. On the one hand this gives you optimal vision[2], and on the other hand dirty glasses create an appearance of negligence."

- "Wear wristwatches to project an air of trustworthiness and a serious concern for punctuality."

- "In Russia, never reject an invitation to the sauna."[3]

---

[2] Wow. Thanks a ton – would *never* have figured this out on my own.

[3] Man oh man, would I get fired for breaking this rule. There are precious few Russian businessmen I'm anxious to get sweaty with.

It's one thing to provide employees with some basic guidelines on dress and behavior, but it's something else entirely to treat them as though they are abjectly incapable of handling even the most trifling details for themselves. Congratulations, UBS! I'm excited to have you tell me what cereal I should eat for breakfast – if that's even permitted, of course!

But mostly, I'm excited to learn about all these illegal tax shelters you're so familiar with. I get a $50 check from my grandma every Christmas, and I'm tired of the government cutting into my profits.

Micromanagement usually functions like it does at UBS, on an institutional level. But never fear – it can be an individual effort as well. You don't have to be part of a giant machine in order to be a world-class micromanager; you can do it all by yourself, without any outside help. You are capable of great things.

And if you do everything right, then maybe you too can one day become as successful a micromanager as Harold Geneen.

Profiles in Tyranny: Harold Geneen

An accountant by training, Harold Geneen was one of the most thoroughly successful micromanagers of the 20th century. When he took over ITT in 1959, the company was focused solely on the foreign telephone market and had less than $800,000 in revenue. Over the next 19 years, he built ITT into a massive international conglomerate with interests in bread, rental cars, grass seed, insurance, hotels, and hundreds of other completely disparate and unrelated fields. If somebody around ITT headquarters were to ask for something – say, "Hey, does anybody have a thumbtack?" – Geneen would stop whatever he was doing, find the largest thumbtack factory in the world, and buy it. Or better yet, he'd buy a mining company, then a construction company, then a plastics manufacturer. That way, he could make his own thumbtacks and have three extra companies to manage!

How did one conglomerate function across so many different industries? Because Geneen controlled *everything*. He gave all his managers overlapping responsibilities – hurray for checks and balances – and then required every one of those managers to provide him with all pertinent information. More than 100 managers delivered reports to Geneen's personal attention every week. In fact, a month before his retirement, the time when most outgoing CEOs are trying to figure out which country club to build their retirement home on, Geneen received 146 reports totaling 2,537 pages, and he read every one of them. And you thought *you* were overworked!

"If I can't solve something," Geneen said, "how the hell can I expect my managers to?"

Exactly, Mr. Geneen. You've hired idiots, which is why you need to be doing everything yourself.

His micromanagement didn't stop there, either. In 1970, under Geneen's direction, ITT funneled $350,000 into Chile to help fund the presidential bid of Jorge Alessandri – or more specifically, to oppose the potential election of Salvador Allende, who was threatening to nationalize an ITT subsidiary based in Chile. Allende won the election, and the ITT subsidiary was nationalized. End of story, right? Wrong! Ever the micromanager, Geneen *then* attempted to micromanage the CIA by offering them $1,000,000 to put pressure on Allende. Seriously, people, the man never quit!

He really didn't. Even after he stepped down as ITT's chief executive he continued to buy and sell companies from his office in Manhattan's Waldorf Astoria Hotel. In fact, even into his 80s Geneen worked a ten-hour day.

But for the best evidence of Geneen's prowess as a micromanager, look no further than these two points:

- **ITT collapsed almost immediately following Geneen's departure!!!**
- **In the month of Geneen's death, ITT was saved from complete dissolution only because it was taken over by another conglomerate!!!**

The conglomerate was simply too big to sustain, and once Geneen was no longer reading 2,500 pages a month and directing every major decision for each of ITT's 350 companies, the whole animal disintegrated. Honestly, can you think of any death as beautiful as this one?

Speaking of death, Geneen's tombstone has an interesting epitaph that epitomizes everything he stood for.

Harold Sydney Green

January 22, 1910 – November 21, 1997

"This grave really should be a few inches to the left."[4]

[4] OK, I made that up. But everything else I said about him is absolutely true.

The story of Harold Geneen leads us to an important point. Like all brilliant micromanagers, Geneen created a working environment so convoluted, unintuitive, and idiosyncratic that it became entirely dependent upon him. It's a quality often seen in comedians, entertainers, and actors, who often strive to develop a 'style' that sets themselves apart from their fellow performers. They pay attention to the minutiae of performing – every gesture, every inflection, every pause. That's why Clint Eastwood is such a unique actor, and why nobody else seems to be able to wag their finger and rant quite like Lewis Black.

But the same skills that benefit a performer almost always create an unstable inequality when applied to a company. Because Geneen was such a prolific and adept micromanager, ITT became more than just a business; it became an extension of Geneen himself. Geneen didn't just put his stamp on ITT – he choked it beneath his bootheel. Which meant that when Geneen left, ITT couldn't survive without him.

So, what is this important point I mentioned a couple paragraphs ago? Here it is. It's one I've alluded to before, and it's one you need to pay careful attention to:

Even the best tyranny rarely lasts longer than the tyrant who created it

That's right, my aspiring tyrant. Military, political, and corporate history are all replete with examples of tyrannies that fell into chaos and disarray upon the death of the tyrant whose vise-like grip was holding everything together.

Alexander the Great's empire lasted exactly nine seconds past his death before being split into four kingdoms, which promptly went to war with each other. The grand, world-encompassing empire that Alexander dreamed of was never to be.

But I'm getting ahead of myself. We'll be covering how to make sure your company goes down with you in a later section.

So you have successfully created an environment of fear, self-interest, and mistrust. You've set the appropriate tone. Your workplace should now be a tense and joyless one, a corporate viper, waiting for its unlucky victim to make a wrong move. The wheels are in motion; your tyranny has begun!

But all we've really done up to this point is atmospheric. Yes, there's a general sense of nervousness and carefully contained misery, but we've just scratched the surface. Now it's time to reach out, to focus on the things you can do to actively oppress and demoralize your workforce. Remember, the tyrant's mantra of employee relations - trample your underlings, then trample them again.

You're about to have a lot of fun.

Trample Your Underlings... Then Trample Them Again

Talk More Than You Listen!

"SHUT UP!!!
SHUT UP!!!
Twenty-five hours, eight days a week
Thirteen months a year is when you speak
I'm tired of listening to the garbage you talk
Why don't you find a short pier, and take a long walk
You talk too much then you never shut up!
You talk too much, tired of hearing you speak
You talk too much Eight days a week
I said you talk too much why don't you ever
SHUT UP!!!"
Run DMC

I am so excited for you! This is the tyrant's bread and butter, the collection of tactics and techniques that will help you make your workplace a dark and unendurable one. I know as a child that you relished the sound of other children crying on the playground. I know you laugh at the "*The Office*" because of the awkward, constant misery of every one of its characters. I know you imagine at least one of your employees every time you're given the opportunity to whack a piñata. And I know you've been waiting for a book like this to help you fully realize your least charitable impulses.

Fun Fact!

Routine work represents approximately 80% of the average person's working day.

This is an important statistic, because it will help you keep this section of the book in proper perspective. I'm going to share a wealth of information with you, and with so many ways to trample your underlings, you might worry that you'll never have time for all of them. But you don't have to. Because most of your employees' workday is already determined for them. The majority of what they do will be the same from day to day, which means that you don't have to dominate their every working moment. You just have to influence that 20% that has the potential to make their day special and glorious - or tedious and unbearable.

Now there really is no culminating moment in this section, no neat summary the way micromanagement was for *Creating an Environment of Fear, Self-Interest, and Mistrust*. So I'm just going to toss ideas out here, and you do all the ones that appeal to you. *Trample Your Underlings...* is a grab-bag of fun, a potpourri of wisdom.

Another Fun Fact!

In a study of 500 mangers in North America, 75% of them reported knowing employees within their company whose unique knowledge would be lost if they left the company.

And you what I say to those people? Good riddance! Glad to see you go, and don't let the door bruise your tailbone on the way out. Those people are a menace to any aspiring tyrant. As I've already pointed out, that 'unique knowledge' could someday become a threat to you, and it's better to see them move to another company than stay around, scheming and plotting your eventual overthrow.

Still Another Fun Fact – the Funnest of Them All!

One study of healthcare workers found that when employees were working for a boss they disliked, they had significantly higher blood pressure. Boss-induced hypertension could increase the risk of coronary heart disease by one-sixth and stroke by one-third. And employees who work for bad bosses for four years or more are 64% more likely to experience a serious heart problem than employees who work for good bosses.

Is that freaking amazing or what? Your tyranny can actually *hasten the death of your employees!* I know you've dreamt of wielding such power before, but I'm sure you despaired of ever acquiring it. But now, it can all be yours!

Getting Down to Business!

As you know, the focus of this section is talking more than you listen. Of everything in the *Trample Your Underlings!* pantheon, this is the quickest way to let your employees know how little you care about what they think. And it also happens to be the easiest thing in the world to do.

How easy? Let me illustrate. As I've mentioned a few times, I have the privilege of speaking at corporate events around the world[1] and teaching people just like yourself how to become a better, more intolerable tyrant. Over the course of those events I've developed a verbal assault that should aptly demonstrate the power of talking more than you listen.

Excerpt from One of My Unbelievably Awesome *Unleash Your Inner Tyrant!* Corporate Presentations

Conference Attendee: "Mr. Havens, can you show me how to talk more than I listen?"

Me: "Excuse me?"

Conference Attendee: "Oh, I'm sorry. I meant, Most Majestic and Magnanimous Havens, Creator of All Things Good in Business, can you show me how to talk more than I listen?"

Me: "That's more like it. And yes I can. But first, tell me, how are you enjoying the conference so far?"

Conference Attendee: (begins to open his mouth)

Me: "I'm loving it myself. We're in a nice hotel, and everybody's been just delightful to me. It's my first time in Boise, too, and I'm telling you, the whole state of Idaho has really done an excellent job

[1] Except for Utah and Delaware. For some reason, nobody in those two states likes me. But that will change someday. Oh yes. Someday, Utah and Delaware shall both be mine.

of fooling the rest of the world into thinking that there's no reason to come here. It's *gorgeous.* Anyway, what do you like to do when you're not working? What are some of your hobbies?"

Conference Attendee: (unbelievably, begins to open his mouth *again*)

Me: "Do you like golf? I don't myself, I'm terrible at it. My brothers are fantastic, but I shoot like a 130. Last time I played I drove the ball directly into a goose's butt. I'm not lying. Most people go for an eagle, I got a goose. Anyway, do you play an instrument or anything? I play the drums myself. Can't believe my parents bought their 10-year old son a drum set, but I thank them for it every day, I think I appreciate music more because of it. But enough of that. What do you think we could do to fix this whole health care thing I keep hearing about? My premiums went up 17% this year, for the second year in a row – and I think we'd all agree that that's unsustainable. So what do you think we can do?"

Conference Attendee: (hesitant to open his mouth)

Me: "No, seriously, I'm curious, what do you think we could do?[2]"

Conference Attendee: "Well, I – "

Me: "Because you know what I think we should do." (At this point, **Conference Attendee** generally

[2] See, that's the other nice thing about talking more than you listen: it keeps people off-balance. They won't know if you want them to speak or shut up, it's *wonderful.*

gives up entirely.) "I think we should just send anyone who doesn't have insurance to prison. Because we have health coverage in prison. It's a weird system, but that's what we have, so why change it? So if it ever happens that I don't have health insurance and need to go to prison to get healed, you know what crime I'm going to commit? Aggravated battery. For two reasons. One, it's a two year sentence in most places, and you can fix most things in two years or at least get a good head start on treatment. But more importantly, there are already a ton of people I would love to beat the crap out of. I can have my cake and eat it too. I'll stay right at the scene of the crime, I will happily be apprehended, go to court and tell the whole truth. 'Why did you assault this man?' 'Well, your honor, because he's a jerk...and I have polyps. Take me away, I'm ready for chemo.'"

Do you see what I've done here? I've completely crushed this conference attendee's desire to offer his or her opinion. It's easy to do. There are only two secrets - one thing you need to do, and another that you only need to understand.

First, the hard part, which really shouldn't be difficult at all: *leverage your positional authority.* In my case, I'm the one who's supposed to be talking. I have the microphone, the lights are on me, people's attention is directed at me, and I use that to my advantage. I tell you, sometimes I wish I could have a stage and an A/V crew with me at all times. Especially when I'm at a bar. I want a drink as much as the next person, but I am just not going to wear a tube top in order to get one.

Profiles in Tyranny: Neil Cavuto, Bill Maher, Bill O'Reilly, and Just About Every Other "News Anchor" on Television

Long ago, in a magical land in a faraway place, there lived a creature called the 'objective news reporter.' This fabled beast was noble and wise, sharing wisdom with its fellow creatures *without offering its own opinion.* It simply stated the things that happened in its lands and among its peoples, and it allowed everyone to form their own opinions based on a collection of objective, indisputable facts. It occasionally conducted interviews with its fellows, and the nobility of the 'objective news reporter' was so great that it usually allowed its interview subjects to speak their minds and finish their thoughts without being interrupted. It was indeed a magical time, and the world was good.

Then global warming came, and the 'objective news reporter' died out. Their extinction was swift and unforeseen, and the vacuum caused by their sudden disappearance allowed for a new creature to emerge – the modern television news pundit.

Pay attention, my aspiring tyrant – if you want to learn how to talk more than you listen, you need look no further than your nearest television. I cannot remember the last time I heard Neil Cavuto allow one of his interview subjects to finish a complete thought, especially if that guest has the nerve and indecency to be a Democrat. Bill Maher's Republican guests are routinely shouted down by himself and his other panel guests, and I've actually seen Bill O'Reilly lunge across the table to shut his guest's microphone off when he didn't like what his guest was saying. That these people are considered news sources is an enormous relief to everyone who prefers to believe what they believe without the inconvenience of contradictory facts or opposing viewpoints. If the 'objective news reporter' were alive today...but again, they're all extinct. Thank God for global warming!

So, how do they get away with it? How is Neil Cavuto so consistently able to talk over his interview subjects? How can Bill Maher so effectively pummel his guests into sullen submission?

Pay close attention, my aspiring tyrant. This is their secret. They know a truth that I am honored to be able to impart to you.

Most people are simply too nice to let you know when you're being a dick.

It's that simple! When I browbeat my conference attendees by talking more than I listen, it's because I know they're not going to put up a fight. They're not going to stand up, shout at me, rail against my tyrannical practices and walk out of the ballroom, because that's not how they were raised. I know that about them, and so I use it against them.

And You Can Too!

Chances are you're already very good at this! To gauge your effectiveness at talking more than you listen, you need to ask yourself one question, and one question only.

When was the last time one of your subordinates directly contradicted you?

That's it! When was the last time one of your employees said specifically that one of your ideas was wrong, misguided, or could be improved? When was the last time one of your employees freely offered a piece of constructive criticism? When was the last time one of your employees initiated a conversation with you about work?

If you can't remember, then chances are you're doing a very good job of talking more than you listen, and I salute you.

So put that one in your pocket, my aspiring tyrant. Pull it over whenever you need to, and soon enough the only voice you'll hear around the office will be your own!

Sucking Like a Champion!

Email Bombardment and Other Annoying Ways to Overcommunicate

Hello, and welcome to another installment of *Sucking Like a Champion!* In this section you will learn how to aggravate everyone around you by drowning them in memos, emails, notices, and other inconsequential pieces of office chatter. I felt that this was the appropriate time to share these tips with you, since we just perfected your ability to talk more than you listen. Following the advice in this bonus section will allow you to continue your verbal monopoly into the written realm, too!

Much of what I'm going to tell you is already being practiced in workplaces everywhere, so this might not seem as amazing and revelatory as some of my other gems. But in case yours is one of the few places where these practices are not already in place, here you go!

- ***Make sure to 'reply all' to EVERY email you receive***
  It should go without saying that everybody in your office should be a part of every conversation that everybody ever has. This will keep everybody constantly informed of everything, and it will warm the hearts of your colleagues when

they log on every morning and find their inbox stuffed full of unimportant minutiae. This, of course, is the absolute opposite of remaining aloof and above and sharing nothing with anybody, but it somehow manages to annoy people just as much as not receiving any information at all. Plus, 'reply all' will allow you the occasional bonus of accidentally copying somebody on something that they *really* shouldn't be seeing – like, for example, how much you really don't like working with them. Think it couldn't happen to you? Just keep hitting 'reply all' and see for yourself!

- ***When in doubt, print it out*** What's this? Your emails keep getting kicked back because your workmates' inboxes are full? Well, that's no problem for a resourceful person like yourself! There's bound to be a copier somewhere nearby – and if not, I'm sure you have a printer right by your desk. You've used it to print off that uninspiring Powerpoint we were talking about in the last *Sucking* section, remember? And like I told you then, if there's one thing everyone needs, *it's more paper!*

- ***Solicit everyone's input*** There are just over 300,000,000 people in the United States, and we have a hard enough time getting 435 representatives and 100 senators to agree on anything. Can you imagine how chaotic things would be if all 300,000,000 had a say on every piece of legislation? Well you don't *have* to imagine it – just ask everybody to offer their opinion on every decision in your workplace, and you'll be able to see democracy in action.

- ***Double up*** So you left a message, huh? Well, maybe they won't ever pick up their phone again. Maybe their phone has been confiscated, or perhaps they left it in their hotel room and the housekeeper accidentally threw it away. You'd better send them an email version of your voicemail message, just to make sure you get through. And after that, you might see if they're on IM. Because maybe your email got accidentally sent to their spam folder. It happens, and you can never be too careful. (This method, by the way, is also a great way to convince a girl to go ahead and file that temporary restraining order she's been contemplating for a while.)

- ***Don't forget the one word responses*** These delicious tidbits of electronic nothing often say 'Thanks!' or 'OK!' Whatever they say, they definitely involve an exclamation point, and they eat a few seconds out of your target's day. Which doesn't really seem like that big a deal, right? But if a hundred other people are doing the same thing…well, let's just say that eating one donut on your break isn't going to bust your belt open either, but if you do it every day…

The art of overcommunication was actually codified back in 1975 in a process known as Brooks' Law. The law is named after Fred Brooks, a software engineer for IBM who realized that the more people that were added to an overdue project, the *longer* it took to complete the project. In other words, adding additional voices to a late project makes that project later. Brooks' Law is organized around two major theses: first, that every person added into a communication channel needs time to be brought up to speed, which eats into the time you could be spending actually doing whatever it is you need to be doing; and second, that while the number of people increases arithmetically, the number of communication channels increases exponentially.

But you don't really need to know *why* it works. You just need to know *that* it works.

So get to work. And make sure to check your voicemail and inbox as soon as you can. I left you a few dozen messages in the last hour. Just wanted to make sure you got them. Let me know as soon as you can – thanks!

Demand the Impossible!

"There is nothing impossible to him who will try."
Alexander the Great

"Accomplishing the impossible means only that the boss will add it to your regular duties."
Doug Larson

Yes! Yes! YES! We are finally to it, one of the cornerstones of unleashing your inner tyrant - demanding the impossible. This has been a hallmark of tyrannical management since employees were invented. Trust me, your subordinates will *hate* this!

Almost 80% of executives and managers do not consider the results expected of them to be realistic for them to deliver – and in companies with more than 10,000 employees, almost 90% feel this way

Isn't that heartwarming? Chances are, you or somebody you know is demanding the impossible on a daily basis.

Your Most Important Weapon...

"But wait a second!" you might be thinking. "I've been told my whole life that nothing is impossible. I've got a picture of the ocean with some smooth rocks and a seagull that somebody gave me to decorate my beige office walls, and it says that nothing is impossible unless you think it's impossible. I've got a coffee cup that somebody gave me for a birthday present because they couldn't think of anything decent to get me for my birthday, and it *also* tells me that my doubts and fears are the only thing keeping me from doing whatever I want. So how can I demand the impossible when everything is apparently possible?"

Don't you see? That's the beauty of this whole thing. Because *plenty* of things are impossible.

Impossible Stuff!

1) Go back and re-read the first quote of this chapter. Did Alexander accomplish the impossible? Did he realize his dream of conquering the entire world? No! Not even close. He didn't even come *close* to conquering Iowa. And the lands that he *did* conquer fell into chaos immediately after he died. I told you that already. Pay attention.

2) Adolf Hitler dreamed of a Third Reich that would last 1,000 years. What happened? He made it 12 years and then crashed in a gigantic ball of flames.

3) When I was kid I truly thought I could duct tape the four corners of a blanket to my arms and legs and then jump off the garage roof and glide across the yard like a flying squirrel. You know what I learned? I learned that gravity is evil and hates us,

and that casts aren't as cool when you're the one wearing them.

And yet we *still* maintain this ridiculous belief that everything is possible. We buy Successories prints and quote Lewis Carroll's 'six impossible things before breakfast' line and try to fool ourselves into believing that nothing is beyond our abilities.

So what does this all mean for you? It means that you can demand the impossible *while simultaneously telling your employees that everything is possible!* It means you can give them absurd assignments and force them to champion undeniably lost causes *while also saying that any failure on their part is a function of their lack of effort!* It's the perfect double-edged sword, my aspiring tyrant, and you need to wield it well if you want to cut your employees' legs out from underneath them.

An Important Distinction

Before we get into how exactly to go about demanding the impossible, it's important to make a distinction between 'demanding the impossible' and 'demanding difficult things that are possible but will require a great deal of work'. The latter is the hallmark of those pathetic fools known as *good leaders*. Those of you who have ever hired a personal trainer or survived basic training in any military branch will know what I'm talking about. Army sergeants are excellent at pushing recruits to do more than they thought they were capable of doing on their own. They yell and scream and threaten – and please, do the same in your tyrannical office,

OK? – but ultimately their goal is to push people past their own self-imposed limits to a more impressive state of being.

Case in point: Barack Obama. Whether you like him or not, the fact that he was able to inspire his political team to help him carry North Carolina and Indiana in the 2008 presidential election – states which hadn't voted for a Democratic presidential candidate since 1976 and 1964 respectively – *that* is an example of a leader demanding a difficult but obviously not impossible task.

And that is absolutely *not* what I'm talking about. When I say impossible, I mean physically or logically impossible.

Example Time!

Let me give you some good 'Demand the Impossible' examples. The following statements were submitted to an Internet contest by employees as actual statements they had heard from their managers.

Seriously, I'm Not Making These Up!

- *"What I need is a list of specific unknown problems we will encounter."*
  Specifically unknown. You want to me to outline and describe things that, by their very nature, are impossible to predict until they happen? I'll get right on that.

- *"E-mail is not to be used to pass on information or data. It should be used only for company business."*

I don't know about you, but my brain just exploded.

- *"This project is so important, we can't let things that are more important interfere with it."*
  Great. Thanks, boss, absolutely, that'll really help me prioritize. So let me get this straight…first we do important things, then we do *really* important things. Maybe I should write this down…

- ***Manager***: *"I need a status report on your project."*
  Employee: *"Sure thing, I'll get it to you tomorrow."*
  Manager: *"If I wanted it tomorrow, I would have waited until tomorrow to ask for it!"*
  This is my personal favorite. Why? Because not only is it impossible, it's also rude and condescending!

You can already see the power of this approach, I can tell. Demanding the impossible is easy, effective, and a world of fun.

However, if you're having trouble figuring out how to take these specific examples and apply them to your particular situation, just keep these general guidelines in mind:

> ***Always ask for things on an impossibly short deadline*** Some of you might have been practicing this one already, especially on your IT department. Contrary to popular belief, computer problems don't actually take 5 seconds to correct. Sometimes it takes more than a simple reboot-and-

restart to resolve the issue. But that's no reason for you to stop demanding your tech support to fix problems the second they occur, is it?

Never look back Proofreading is for idiots, and logical consistency is for people with too much time on their hands and not enough to do. If you are pausing mid-sentence to thoughtfully consider your words, you are committing a sin against the Tyrant's Code. Besides, if somebody doesn't understand what you're saying, isn't it their fault for not trying hard enough to figure out exactly what you mean? You can't spell everything out everybody, can you – if you did, how would you ever get any work done?

Sometimes change your requirements It's important not to do this all the time, lest your employees figure out your M.O. and start doing the opposite of everything you ask for in anticipation of the 180 you're about to pull on them. As long as you're only *occasionally* giving contradictory orders, you'll be able to keep your employees in a constantly frustrating state of uncertainty. Woo-hoo!

Demand Perfection...But Don't Allow for a Learning Curve!!!!

This is a delightful variation on demanding the impossible. Demanding perfection is not necessarily the province of a tyrant. In fact, many industries require near-perfection. Most machined parts today allow for deviations of less than a millimeter, while deviations in the computing industry are often less than a micrometer. Surgery, bridge building, pharmaceuticals - these are just a few of the examples of industries in which perfection is often the standard rather than the goal.[1]

However, perfection is the result of years of dedicated practice. I'm sure you've heard of the 10,000-hour rule, based on a study by Anders Ericsson and made popular in Malcolm Gladwell's book *Outliers*, which argues that people must spend 10,000 hours at a given task before becoming experts. Indeed, in another study, Dr. Benjamin Bloom of Northwestern University found that regardless of profession, it takes between 10 and 18 years to achieve world-class abilities.

Which of course is why you need to demand perfection *now*!!!

Make no mistake: the fact that your employees are young, inexperienced, new to the company, working on a new kind of project, or dealing with a nascent form of technology is no excuse for them to not already know how to do everything. Would you like a maxim to follow? Here it is:

Learning takes time.
Time is money.
So you need to let your employees know
how much money they're wasting by learning!!!

---

[1] "Wait a second! You left out government!" Yes. Yes I did. That was intentional.

Think about it. Every time your employees open a book to consult a training manual or look up a fact, they're spending time that could better be spent on making you money. Every time they stop to think before acting, they're costing your company a fortune in lost production time.

Besides, think of it this way. You had to learn a lot to get to the position that you're currently in, didn't you? Absolutely you did. And you know what will happen if you allow your employees time to learn? They'll eventually know how to do things well. Worse, they might *realize* that they're good at stuff, and then what'll happen? Revolution, that's what'll happen! They'll start demanding perks, promotions, special consideration, and who knows what else.

So, how do you start demanding perfection without allowing for a learning curve? Well, I like to begin this particular tyrannical approach with a little game.

Tyranny in Three Easy Steps!

1) Pick an employee at random. Or, better yet, choose an employee who has irritated you recently. Possible reasons for irritation:

    a. Looked you directly in eye when talking to you
    b. Recently received a commendation from another manager in your company
    c. Ate the last piece of coffeecake in the breakroom
    d. Seems a little too happy with things
    e. Has more attractive children than you do

2) Hand your target a Rubik's Cube.

3) Tell them to solve it in a minute. Assure them that you're not joking when they laugh at your request, then stare at them while they work.

This is a little game I like to play during my leadership seminars, and it never fails to bring the point home. As your employee struggles to appease your impossible demand, one of two things will happen:

- He or she might attempt to solve the puzzle but will only give it a halfhearted effort and, more importantly, will hate every moment of the assignment because you will have put him/her in an impossible situation.
- He or she won't even try at all.

Either way, your employees will end that minute frustrated, annoyed, deflated, and angry because you will have made them feel incompetent because you gave them an unreasonable task. And that's perfect.

And then, open the floodgates! Demand status reports on an impossibly short time frame; require employees to master new software over the weekend; expect new sales associates to close a major account in their first week on the job; buy everyone Rosetta Stone and tell them to learn Japanese by lunch. The harder the task, the less time you should give people to complete it.

And if you've done everything right, then maybe you can one day be like this…

Storytime!

Annaliese met the worst boss of her life when she was 19, while studying Hotel and Restaurant Management in Germany.

"While going to school I worked in a hotel as a trainee to earn money and get some practical experience. One day my Cost Accounting class had a guest teacher, the founder of a German consulting company. I was so impressed by him that I quit my training job and started working for him. He was opening a healthy fast-food restaurant in a local mall, and I was tasked with tending to the office work, marketing and accountancy. My new boss told me that I would learn so much from him that I'd be able to run my own company in less than a year."

Ridiculous promises of impossible wealth and power? Sounds too good to be true! Let's find out what happens...

"I got no training. None of us did. My boss was busy managing his other companies in Berlin, Munich, and China. Two weeks after I started, the restaurant manager disappeared. Three days later his assistant vanished. They were older and apparently knew what was going to happen. I was left with 10 insecure, nervous employees. I'd worked 1 year as an au pair and half a year in a hotel kitchen, so I knew how to bottle-feed infants and cut tomatoes. What I didn't know was how to be a manager. I had no clue! In less than a month I was working 90 hours a week."

Sounds like a heck of a strain! Surely your boss helped you find replacements for the manager and his assistant?

"Absolutely not," Annaliese says. "He put *me* in charge of finding a new store manager and of firing some of the employees for him, since he was 'too busy with his other companies'. It was a disaster! *And* there was no money in the company's bank account; I wasn't able to pay the bills or any of the employees. So once a month, I had to beg my boss for money – asking wasn't enough, I had to beg him."

"I first showed signs of burnout – at the age of 20!!!! – while my boss went on vacation to France. I wasn't – "

Wait a second, Annaliese. Your boss went *on vacation* while you, a completely untrained marketing assistant, tried to run a restaurant without a full staff or any of the knowledge necessary to do your job well?

"That's right. Every time I entered the mall and saw the company logo, I started to cry. I was enormously underweight, and eventually I ended up collapsing. My boss had to come back from France to take care of things. After I recovered he did a good job on making my feel guilty about the messed up vacation."

Wow. I should have gotten his guy to write this chapter for me!

"After getting my bachelor's degree I started working as a casino manager and have been quite successful. There still is no day since working for this horrible person that I don't think about what a nightmarish experience that was. I've imagined many times what I would do or say if I ever saw him again, but none of that is printable. I will say this, though: his being the worst boss ever taught me how to be good one."

Now I'm sure some of you have heard that 90% of knowledge is failure. Perhaps you know that Thomas Edison allegedly burned through 1,000 failed light bulb designs before finally hitting upon a commercially viable one. Perhaps you know that Sir Thomas Dyson, inventor of the Dyson vacuum and other products (including that weird 255 mph Air Blade thing you see in airport bathrooms now), allegedly failed more than 5,000 times before finding his particular success. Perhaps you know that Sony's original name (Tokyo Tsushin Kogyo KK) and its original product (a rice cooker) were both complete and utter failures, and that Sony somehow managed to push through those failures to find some modest success in the business world (~$34 billion market capitalization, give or take twelve dollars). Perhaps you've synthesized this and other information, processed it in what passes for your brain, and have come to believe that some amount of failure is essential if you want to build and grow and become better.

And I disagree. Good people, good companies, good relationships, *never fail*.

And now you're probably thinking, "That doesn't make any sense. In fact, that statement directly contradicts every example you used in the previous paragraph." And you're right. It doesn't make sense. And it doesn't have to.

Why? The answer, my aspiring tyrant, is the title to our next chapter.

Create Double Standards

"We don't pay taxes. Only the little people pay taxes."
Leona Helmsley

If you're like most people, the very subject of this chapter should be making your skin crawl. I'm certain you've been on the receiving end of a double standard before, and so I'm sure you know how truly devious and hateful they are. This is unquestionably the most annoying tool in the entire *Unleash Your Inner Tyrant!* program, which of course is why you should pay very careful attention. If you want to trample your underlings and suck all the joy out of their working life, this single technique is just the ticket.

Before we get started, take a moment to revisit the opening quote to this chapter. It's a rather famous one, certainly the sentences for which Leona Helmsley is most famous. They are the ten little words that cemented this one-time billionaire heiress in the public mind as one of the world's most openly heartless people. Seriously, I've seen pictures of her, and I'm not sure she was cute even as a baby. They're the words that help explain why she was so unloved upon her death that she was forced to leave a considerable portion of her fortune to her cat.

Repeat them to yourself. Whisper them as you fall asleep. They shall be your mantra, and guide you through the darkness.

Some Mighty BIG Examples!

So, let's start with some big examples of double standards and work our way down.

First – Soviet Communism. I could just as well discuss communism in general, but the Soviet model is the easiest one to describe.[1] Communism, if you'll remember, was a philosophical reaction against the excesses and abuses of autocratic rule. A movement of and for the common people, it was designed to correct the unsustainable inequities of a feudal system in which the vast majority of Russia's wealth and privilege was concentrated in the hands of an extremely small number of people. Soviet Communism envisioned a uniform equality, a utopian society in which all members were equally valuable and thus equally rewarded.

This equality, I believe, is most delightfully evidenced by the architectural and aesthetic similarities between the typical Soviet-era apartment building…

[1] The Chinese version of Communism, with its haphazard embrace of capitalist economics and arbitrary currency valuation, is such a confusing beast that I can make no sense of it. Fortunately, neither can they.

...and Meiendorf Castle, home of the Russian President.

Ah, yes. They seem equally well-appointed. It would hardly matter to me which one I got to live in.

Way to go, Soviet Communism! It's one thing to facilitate an unequal distribution of wealth, but it's quite another to do so while promising not to do so!

But my current favorite double standard is a bit closer to home - namely, the U.S. banking system, which has concocted a beautiful double standard in the different lending rates that individuals and banks are subjected to. The average person, as you may already know, is able to borrow money from a bank at somewhere between four and fifteen percent interest. The average *bank*, however, is able to borrow money from the government at an interest rate currently near *zero*.

Allow that to sink in. Do you know what I could do if I could borrow $10 million, or $1 million, or even $500,000 at 0% interest? Why, I think I'd be rich! I could invest it *risk-free*!!! But they won't let me.

Thanks a lot, banks.

Some Mighty COMMON Examples!

Now this of course is what a good tyrant is shooting for – systemic differences in the rules and rewards that govern different populations. But although I've started off with some pretty sizeable examples, you can create double standards on a much smaller scale as well. And the good thing is, you probably already have!

Things I Hope You're Already Doing!

- ***Recognizing key milestones for some employees and not others***
  All of your employees have birthdays, but only some deserve to be acknowledged. The same goes for anniversaries, years of service, and anything else that might be cause for recognition. Remember – just because somebody's been with you for fifteen years doesn't mean you should make a big deal out of it. The fact that you still pay them should be gratitude enough.

- ***Saying hello only to select people as you walk past***
  This will be significantly easier if you don't bother to learn all of your employees' names.

- ***Only providing your 'important' employees with minor amenities***
  I don't care what you call these people – 'star players,' 'top talent,' 'people too popular for me to fire,' e.g. – as long as you distinguish their

supremacy through the use of inconsequential perks. It's one thing to award a bonus to your top salesperson, which can conceivably be viewed as an incentive for your other salespeople to strive for more success. But it's quite another to withhold business cards or extended lunch breaks from everyone who has not yet achieved elite status. The more tiers you can put in place, the more divisions you'll create between the members of your workforce. And you know how I feel about divisions.[2]

- ***Using different words to describe similar behaviors!!!!***

This last one is a phenomenal technique, and probably the most popular of them all. It has the triple advantages of being simple, subtle, and sustainable. You can engage in verbal double standards all day, every day, for as long as you're alive.

How you go about this will depend upon your particular style. If you want your verbal abuse to function like a sledgehammer to the skull, you'll engage in flagrant and obvious double standards, such as referring to male employees as 'sport' or 'champ' and female employees as

[2] My favorite example of this is the airline industry's policy of allowing its elite fliers to walk on the special carpet as they board the plane. Letting them board the plane first – that seems like a tangible reward for their continued loyalty and business. Letting them walk on a $20 squidge of blue carpet and preventing everyone else from doing so? Well, that seems like a completely pointless smack in the face to all the non-elites. It's not a double standard, but it is weird.

'sweetheart,' 'babe,' or 'toots.' This double standard was enormously popular in the 1940s and 50s, and for you to do it properly you'll need to wear a three-piece suit, purchase a fedora, develop a taste for stiff martinis, and smoke a carton of unfiltered cigarettes every day. You'll probably be dead soon, but that should be no reason to stop you.

If you prefer a more devious modern approach, however, you'll use the kinds of understated wordplay that so many tyrants before you have employed:

Hope this Doesn't Hit Too Close to Home!!!

ASSERTIVE VS. AGGRESSIVE

A STRAIGHT TALKER VS. **RUDE**

GREGARIOUS VS. CHATTY

A GO-GETTER VS. **PUSHY**

A MESSY DRESSER VS. NOT CONCERNED ENOUGH ABOUT APPEARANCES

A RISK-TAKER VS. **IMPULSIVE**

DETERMINED VS. BITCHY

Now, you'll notice that while I've organized these terms by column, I haven't said *how* they're organized. Perhaps I've done it by gender, or race, or age, or nationality. But it doesn't matter. The important thing is, you need to ensure that different employees fit into different categories. If you have some employees that fall onto the left side and others that fall onto the right, then congratulations! You're already working toward the kind of unfair and biased environment that your unfortunate subordinates are guaranteed to eventually hate.

The Next Level

But double standards are so much more than fostering a lopsided and imbalanced verbal exchange with your employees. The sky's the limit here, and every inequity you can create is one more bucket of sand with which to fill your tyrannical sandbox.

Kathleen D. Ryan and Daniel K. Oestereich conducted interviews in hundreds of companies to discover what issues employees felt were 'undiscussable' and found 'management practices' constituted 49% of the total

Doesn't that just warm the place where your heart is supposed to be? It should. It goes without saying that you should feel free to criticize your employees as often as you think to.[3] But that does not at all mean that they should feel free to criticize you. Managers have to complain about the way employees work, or else improvement will never happen. But employees should never complain about the way managers manage. If they do, they'll eventually adopt airs and forget their place. And where is their place again? That's right - *beneath you*. They're the feet, remember? Dirty, smelly

[3] We'll actually be covering this more thoroughly in the next chapter, *Focus on the Negatives!* Fun times are ahead!

feet. Re-read *Establish Positional Dominance* if you need a refresher.

In order to perfect the double standard, you'll need to understand that communication is not a two-way street. I know you might have heard otherwise, but whoever said so is an idiot. And how do I know that? Because if they had any intelligence at all, they would have written this book before me.

Need an example? Probably not. But I'm going to give you one anyway.

Storytime!

Felicity worked at an upscale bar and nightclub. If you've ever been to an upscale bar or nightclub, you'll know that there is often an air of class and gentility that suggests a smoothly-run business. Unfortunately for Felicity – but fortunately for this book – her manager did not possess class, gentility, common decency, or a sense of fair play.

"I don't even know where to start," Felicity says. "Most of his employees believe that he may actually be bipolar. He stressed teamwork amongst his managers but complained when some of us became friends because we might cover for each other. He preached and screamed about cutting labor costs but then kept an extra doorman on the clock to sit next to his car so that it didn't get vandalized – which by the way was never a problem of ours."

So far, so good! Anything more?

"Plenty. Remember him screaming at us about cutting labor costs? Well, apparently that didn't apply to having some of us drive his friends home *from other nightclubs* if they'd had too much to drink. There were other things, too – he constantly belittled his managers in front of the rest of the staff and then complained that he didn't get the respect he deserved. I eventually quit when I was told to call him, did so, and then was told quite harshly that he didn't have time to talk to me and that I had lied about being told to call him. That's just one example, though; I have enough stories about him to write a book of my own."

Whoa. Hold on there, Felicity. This chapter's about double standards, not lying. We'll get to the chapter about lying in just a little while.

"But he lied all the time."

I know he did, Felicity. All good tyrants do.

And speaking of good tyrants…drum roll, please!

Profiles in Tyranny:
Angelo Mozilo

Angelo Mozilo is most famously known as a man who should seriously consider canceling his weekly appointment at the tanning salon. But he's almost as famously known as the founder and CEO of Countrywide Financial, the company that came to epitomize the subprime debacle which threw America into the worst recession since the Great Depression of the 1930s. So in a weird way, Countrywide Financial was probably the best name for a company Mozilo could have ever come up with. Because he helped to make sure that everybody suffered across the entire country!

Everyone but him, of course.

Oh, and his friends – did I forget them? How silly of me! After all, that's the crux of his genius as a double standard bearer. Mozilo had a two-tiered lending system: a regular one at regular market lending rates for regular people who couldn't do anything useful for him; and a special one with below-market lending rates for lawmakers, politicians, and others who had the ability to help Countrywide with favorable legislation.

But if you think the double standards stop there, think again! Have you ever heard the phrase, "Kill one man, you're a murderer – kill a thousand, and you're a conqueror?" Well, the same conceit apparently applies to financial misconduct as well. Mozilo was ultimately forced to pay a $67.5 million fine for insider trading and securities fraud – roughly 10% of his estimated $600 million net worth. This settlement allowed him – guess what? – to avoid any admission of wrongdoing! How freaking sweet is that?

What's the double standard here? Allow me to answer your question with another question: do you suppose that a common thief would receive such a favorable deal from the authorities? Do you think that someone who stole a car would only be asked to return 10% of that car to its owner *and* also manage to avoid jail time? I don't think so!

I think the lesson is pretty obvious, my aspiring tyrant. If you're going to engage in insider trading, make sure to do it up BIG.

Oh, and make sure to friend request a few politicians on Facebook or something. Those connections can go a long way.

So there you have it! Consistency is for fools - or more accurately, for people who don't want to become tyrants.

But if there's any problem with double standards, it's that they take a long time to fully bear fruit. Your employees won't recognize for a while that you're treating all of them differently; they might suspect it early on, but it'll take weeks or months for the practice to become obvious and unpleasant. And I know that you might want to establish your tyranny more quickly than a well-planned double standard campaign will allow for.

Which is why I've written the next chapter. It's something you can put into practice immediately, if you're not too stupid to understand it.

Was that too mean? Did I make you cry? Good. That was my objective. And if you think *that's* bad, turn the page!

Focus on the Negatives!!!

"To call you stupid would be an insult to stupid people! I've known sheep that could outwit you. I've worn dresses with higher IQs. Now let me correct you on a couple of things, OK? Aristotle was not Belgian. The central message of Buddhism is not 'Every man for himself.' And the London Underground is not a political movement. Those are all mistakes, Otto. I looked them up."
Wanda, "A Fish Called Wanda"

Ah, we've finally come to it - one of my favorite ways to trample your underlings. A tyrant is never happy. Things could always be better, and you need to communicate your constant disappointment at every opportunity. After all, if your employees were any good at anything, they wouldn't be beneath you on the org chart, would they?

Fortunately for us, there's actually a mathematical model we can use here to help you learn exactly how best to focus on the negatives. Tyranny is usually more of an art than a science, so I'm pleased to be able to provide my left-brained readers with a logical, straightforward, scientific way to make your employees wish they'd trusted their instincts when they thought about refusing the job you offered them.

And here it is. Get out your slide rules and protractors, my diligent reader. Because when it comes to focusing on the negatives, tyranny has a formula.

The Formula!

For this section we are going to focus on the work of John Gottman, a psychology professor at the University of Washington who published a book in 1995 called *Why Marriages Succeed or Fail*. Although the book was intended to focus on marital relationships, the principles have been applied to all manner of relationships, both personal and professional. There's a lot of information in the book, but Gottman's central argument is this:

The ideal ratio of
positive to negative communication,
the ratio healthy and successful relationships
should strive for, is *5-to-1*.

In other words, for every negative thing you say to another person - every critical, demeaning, constructive, or otherwise imperfect sentence that tumbles out of your venomous mouth - you will eventually need to say five nice things to offset it. Gottman also postulated that marriages (and by extension all relationships) which function on a 1-to-1 or 2-to-1 ratio are almost guaranteed to fail.

Now I know what you're thinking. "Big whoop, psychology guy. I could make up a weird ratio too if I felt like it. Anybody can invent numbers. I could say that 83% of statistics are made up. I could say that 95% of Galapagos iguanas die before their fourth birthday, that walruses shed an average of 142 pounds of skin over the course of a year, or that the average person will eat 12 times their own weight in

Denny's pancakes throughout the course of their lifetime. I can make up stupid crap with the best of them. But nobody'd believe me, so why should I believe you?"[1]

Here's why. To test his hypothesis, Gottman and his associates interviewed 700 newly married couples for 15 minutes each. He videotaped the interviews and later wrote down the number of positive communications each couple shared with one another, as well as the number of negative communications. Then, using only this 15-minute interview and his 5-to-1 hypothesis, Gottman predicted which of these couples would stay married and which would get divorced.

Ten years later, he interviewed the same couples. And it turns out that his predictions were accurate ***94% of the time***.

To put that into perspective, keep this in mind: Gottman didn't know these couples. He wasn't their psychologist, he hadn't watched the evolution of their relationships. He met each of them for exactly 15 minutes, and he was able to say with astonishing accuracy which of them were in healthy relationships based on nothing more than a mathematical ratio. That's why this 5-to-1 rule is probably a good ratio to use to gauge the health of your personal and professional relationships.[2]

---

[1] I don't know if that pancakes thing is true or not, but I sure hope it is. Pancakes are *delicious*.

[2] Other researchers have expanded on Gottman's findings and made some interesting observations of their own. Workgroups where the positive-to-negative ratios are above 3:1 are more productive than those that are below 3:1. They've also found what seems to be an upper limit. If the positive-to-negative is 13:1, productivity begins to falter, presumably because everybody is trying so hard to be constantly polite that there aren't enough conversations about the things that legitimately need to be improved.

Does this mean you can't ever have a conversation with someone you care about that focuses entirely on problems or things that need to improve? Does this mean you can't occasionally have a conversation where the positive-to-negative ratio is 3-to-1, or 1-to-6, or 0-to-40? Of course not. Those conversations will happen from time to time. In fact, they have to happen if there are serious issues that need to be addressed and worked out. It just means that, on average and over the course of the relationship in question, you should say five times as many positive things as you do negative things if you want that relationship to be vibrant, healthy, strong, and all those other happy adjectives that people use to describe vibrant, healthy, and strong things.

Perhaps you were familiar with this study and have been attempting to put it into practice with your family and friends. And I encourage you to do so. Even the cruelest tyrants aren't tyrants to their family and friends. I want you to have happy and healthy relationships with your husband, wife, children, siblings, and anybody else that brings your life meaning and joy.

But I also want you to be able to trample your underlings really, really, really well. So do whatever you want to when it comes to your personal relationships. When it comes to your *professional* relationships, however, here's what you should do.

Don't Do This

Here's the deal. A 'good' leader, those poor misguided souls, might take the Gottman study to heart and have a conversation with a subordinate along these lines:

Stupid Conversation I'm Embarrassed to Write

Boss: "Hey, Jim, I'd like to talk with you about the Parker project."

Jim: "Sure. What about it?"

Boss: "Well, a few things. First, you did a very good job with it (+1). You met the deadline (+2), you came in at budget (+3), and your presentation skills have really improved in the last four months (+4)."

Jim: "Thanks!"

Boss: "Sure. Happy to tell you, since it's all true. There is one thing, though, that I'd like you to work on for the next project. I didn't feel like you communicated as effectively with me as you could have (-1). I didn't always feel like I knew where we stood on things. But overall, very well done (+5). So keep up the good work, and just try to think about that for next time."

You can see the 5-to-1 ratio here. And hopefully you can appreciate that while you certainly heard the criticism, it doesn't feel too heavy. In fact, it almost sounds like a genuinely constructive conversation, primarily positive but still with a direct suggestion for future improvement. You can almost see the employee nodding in agreement as he/she listens. These kinds of conversations happen all the time in business across America, and the knowledge of that never fails to make me feel a little nauseous. You ever eat at a bad ethnic restaurant? That's how this conversation makes me feel.

So, now that you know what *not* to do, let's talk about the approach you should take.

Do This!!!

Now it would be easy for me to recommend that you never say a single nice thing to your employees. Too easy, in fact. Of course you can do that. You can pummel them into submission with a relentless assault of criticism and negativity. You can attack their every mistake and ignore or downplay their every success. I shouldn't even need to be writing this.

But that approach, while effective, is also sophomoric. It's the technique of a schoolyard bully, a street thug, hardly befitting a person of your stature. A tyrant might conquer through brute force, but it shouldn't be the only weapon at your disposal.

Which is why I bring to you....the compliment sandwich.

For those of you unfamiliar with the compliment sandwich, it is an ingenious tool of subtle psychological warfare. This 2-to-1 ratio of positive to negative *appears* to be an honest attempt to cushion the pain of a critical comment by covering either end with favorable things. However, the compliment sandwich *actually* serves only to convince your employees that the compliments – the 'bread' of the sandwich, the parts with no nutritional value that we occasionally throw away to avoid the excess calories – are just your cover for the real purpose of the conversation, which is the juicy, succulent, chicken tender of criticism in the middle.

Want some examples? I'm glad you asked. I just so happen to have collected several fantastic examples from attendees at my various communications, change management, and leadership seminars. Who knows? Perhaps you're the one who said them. If so, please get in touch with me so that I can thank you personally for making this chapter such an easy one to write.

Real-Life Examples of the Compliment Sandwich!!!

1) "Thank you for turning in your self-appraisal on time. I must say, your performance this quarter leaves something to be desired. But it sure is a lot better than your performance last quarter!"
2) "Hey, it's great to see you back at your desk….finally."[3]
3) "First off, I want to thank you for being so understanding during the downsizing. Unfortunately, it's been decided to cut your

[3] This one's really a 1:1, not 2:1 ratio, but I like it, so I kept it in. Think of it as an open-faced compliment sandwich.

position. However, I will be happy to write you a very strong recommendation letter."[4]

4) "You've been doing a really good job lately. So good, in fact, that you're actually making the rest of your team look bad. So please, keep up the good work! Just do less of it."

Now, what do you think the focus of all of these exchanges is? What do you think your employees are going to remember? The criticism, of course! Which is exactly why you need to be using the compliment sandwich.

But there's a larger strategy at work here, which I alluded to a moment ago. The compliment sandwich is an excellent way to focus on the negatives while creating the illusion of being nice and thoughtful. Your employees will have a difficult time calling you to task for being overbearing and hypercritical when you can very easily contradict them by pointing to all the so-called 'compliments' that you keep showering them with.

A 1925 study by Dr. Elizabeth Hurlock examined the effects of different kinds of feedback on student achievement. She created three groups of 4th and 6th grade math students; one group was only praised for good work, one only criticized for bad work, and one was ignored. Students in both the first and second groups did better after the first day. In subsequent days, however, their performances changed

[4] O-U-C-H. Just kick me in the teeth while you're at it.

dramatically. By end of 5 days, the first group had improved 71%, the second group had improved 19%, and the third group improved 5%.

There are a couple lessons to learn here. First, the world was a much more wonderful place in 1925, since it was apparently perfectly acceptable to experiment on children. Seriously, people, they are an endlessly renewable resource; why aren't we using them?

Second, praise looks to be four times more effective at facilitating personal improvement than criticism does. But I want you to ignore that. It's extraneous data.

Third, and most importantly for the purposes of this book, criticism is four times better than doing nothing. So don't just sit there doing nothing, people - get out there and start criticizing!

Where's the Profile in Tyranny?

Unfortunately, I don't have a Profile in Tyranny for this section. The closest I could think of was General Patton, who was famous for his volcanic and none-too-delicate tirades about anything that annoyed him (which, from what I can gather, was everything). But that doesn't seem fair. War is a different animal, and yelling at people in the middle of a war is pretty standard. I suppose you could channel Patton while you're in the office, or hire a drill sergeant to wander through your office and proxy your displeasure at 120db.

I do, however, have a real-life story, culled from the annals of the modern corporate world, that will hopefully illustrate the benefits of focusing on the negatives.

Storytime!

Rachel K. was an adjunct professor at a small university. The university was young and growing, and she was hired in August as a part-time teacher with the understanding that she would have the opportunity for full-time employment after her first year.

"I had no reason to expect there would be any problems," Rachel says. "The woman who hired me seemed like the nicest person in the world."

In November, however, near the end of her first semester of teaching, Rachel's supervisor – the same woman who had hired her – called her in to discuss her student evaluations. Apparently they were a bit low. "She told me that my student evals were at 3.9 (out of 5) and that their university expected all its teachers to receive a 4.35 or better," Rachel says.

Seems reasonable, right? Only problem was, her supervisor's criticism wasn't accurate.

"I was hoping for a full-time job, so I made sure to pay attention to what the university wanted from me," Rachel says. "According to their guidelines, all returning teachers were expected to receive a 4.35 or better, but *first-year* teachers were allowed a 3.5. I was actually doing *better* than expected, but she decided that she didn't like me for some reason, so she changed the rules."

A few weeks later, Rachel's supervisor told her that Rachel's students were so dissatisfied with Rachel's teaching that they had all gathered at a meeting to formalize their complaints and present them to the dean.

"She told me this meeting had taken place in October," Rachel says. "I asked why I was only learning about it in November, and she didn't have an answer. I also asked if she'd attended it, and she said that she had not, but that she was still positive all of my students had been there. You have to understand, I was teaching at a nontraditional school – my students had jobs and children and families and irregular schedules. The odds of them all deciding to meet outside of class, or even being able to coordinate their schedules so that they *could* meet, were pretty slim."

But the real kicker came when Rachel was searching online for a potential new job when she came across an interesting job opening: her current job. Apparently her supervisor had decided to post her position without saying anything.

"I submitted my letter of resignation about a week after that," Rachel says. "My boss said exactly two words to me between receiving my letter and my last day: good morning. At least they were nice words."

I know, I know – posting a job opening for a job that isn't open (without telling the person whose job you're posting, by the way) isn't strictly a 'focus on the negatives' issue. But it's such a great example of tyrannical behavior that I just had to mention it. I suppose I could have included this story in the upcoming chapter about lying, but I put it here. It's my book, and I can do what I want.

But that's neither here nor there. The point is, congratulations, O Tyrant of Academia! I'm sure you'll find plenty of problems with Rachel's replacement, too. And if you don't, you can just invent some!

It's a beautiful world, my aspiring tyrant. So get out there and start complaining!

Hopefully that story inspires you to ramp up your own criticism and negativity.

But I think it's time for a change of pace. Enough with the formulas and ratios and mathematical gobbledygook. Time to get crazy for a moment – literally!

But first…bonus chapter time!

Sucking Like a Champion:

Orchestrating a Pointless Meeting

Welcome back to another installment of *Sucking Like a Champion!* In this section we will discuss the five cardinal rules for conducting an ineffective meeting. If used correctly, these techniques can help make your meetings the most dreaded part of your team's working day. In some cases, you've been following this advice your entire career. And if that's the case, I hope that you feel a little swell of pride at the knowledge that you (and others like you) have been the inspiration for this section.

We've all attended pointless meetings before. I attended one meeting so bad that I honestly would have preferred to gouge my own eyes out with a blunt pencil - and I would have done it, too, if the manager in question hadn't cut back on the purchase of pencils in a misguided effort to save money. Note to managers: your exorbitant pencil budget is not the reason you're missing your profit targets for the year.

So without further adieu - in fact, without any adieus at all, because I don't know what 'adieu' means - I present to you the five components of an ineffective meeting:

Step one: Start late. Doing so will convince your team that the meeting they're about to sit through is not even important enough for *you* to attend.

Five minutes late is fine, fifteen minutes is better, and if you can hold off for fifty minutes…pat yourself on the back. There is a hint of tyranny here too, as it presupposes that your employees have nothing more important to do than wait for you, mouths open and palms moist in breathless anticipation of hanging on your every belated word. Throwing off everyone else's schedule just because you can't keep to your own is a special kind of torture, and I'm proud of those of you who have already discovered it.

Step two: Have no clear agenda. There's nothing quite as special – and by 'special' I mean 'maddeningly useless' – as a meeting leader who leaps from topic to topic without any real idea of how they connect or which subjects actually matter. This is the hallmark practice of managers who schedule meetings for no other reason than a vague sense that it's about time to be having another meeting, which I know I've mentioned before, but it's fun so I'm mentioning it again. These meetings are by definition haphazard, and they usually end by accomplishing little more than solidifying the hitherto-unspoken belief that the meeting leader has no real idea what's going on. Plus, it'll be fun for you to watch your subordinates sputter and stumble when you ask them to present their status reports to the rest of the team, which they would have been fully prepared to do if you'd told them to prepare for it.

Step three: Encourage the use of smartphones. This is a relatively new development in the history of the bad meeting, but it's such a powerful tool that it would be criminal for me to overlook it. When it comes to smartphones, there are only two truths you need to understand:

- **Everybody sincerely believes that they are masters at multitasking**
- **Everybody is wrong**

It is impossible to take a phone call, send a text, check email, search the Internet, *and* pay full attention to the particulars of the meeting you're attending. Smartphones have turned most meetings little more than a collection of people in a room all following their own individual pursuits, which of course is why you need to encourage your workers to use theirs.[1] But why should they have all the fun? Pull your phone out mid-sentence and send a text that you forgot to send earlier! It will provide your meeting attendees with the appropriate message – your meeting is worthless, and they would be better served to work on other things.

Step four: Finish late. You should be noticing a time-management theme here, and we've already

[1] Or at the very least, fail to discourage them from using theirs, which amounts to the same thing.

covered how your inability to keep to the time that you established for your own meeting will annoy your underlings. But there's an extra special bonus that comes with finishing late. Sure, it inconveniences everybody and throws an unnecessarily unpleasant crimp into their day. But it will also allow those of your team members with other appointments a legitimate excuse to leave your meeting early. Plenty of them will have phone calls to make, clients to meet, planes to catch, deadlines to…well, you get the idea. Which means they'll miss some of your most important points and be 'out of the loop,' which will necessitate – what else? – *another meeting!*

Step five: Save your most important items for last. Half of your team has left, and the other half is thoroughly disenchanted – the *perfect* opportunity for you to drop whatever bombshells you've been storing up. Mergers, impending layoffs, vague references to 'big changes' on the horizon – pull out the whole arsenal, and watch your employees seethe and squirm like the angry, caged animals you've turned them into!

There you have it – sheer unadulterated brilliance. And it can all be yours. Make every meeting feel like a kick in the teeth. I know you are capable of greatness. Prove it to me.

Threaten Physical Violence!

"Democracy don't rule the world
You'd better get that in your head
This world is ruled by violence
But I guess that's better left unsaid."
Bob Dylan

About time, don't you think? Everything we've talked about up to this point has been designed to exact a psychological toll on your employees. Some are subtle, and some are not. But all of them have dealt with breaking your subordinates' spirit, will, and hope.

Which begs the question, *why stop there?* Your employees have bodies too, don't they? No reason to leave those untouched. After all, it's one thing for your employees to fear for their job and professional future. But it's quite another altogether to make them fear for their life.

95% of employees report that supervisors have become angry with them, 80% say it affects their work, and 75% report that they themselves have become angry with their employees

If that doesn't make you double over with maniacal laughter, I don't know what will.

Before We Get Started, An Important Announcement

All right. I know what some of you are thinking, so let me make myself clear. I am *not* advocating sexual harassment. Most tyrants have their limits, and that's one of mine. Although apparently that's not the case for plenty of other people. A 1980 survey of federal employees found that 42% of women and 15% of men had experienced some form of work-related sexual harassment; in 1987, the same survey found nearly identical results. In 2007, 12,510 sexual harassment grievances were filed with the Equal Employment Opportunity Commission - and since it's estimated that only 5-15% of people actually bother to file a complaint, the real number of sexual harassment incidents is likely in the hundreds of thousands every year.

Why do I disapprove of sexual harassment? It's not because I care about people, because I quite clearly don't. Part of my problem is that it's really expensive and can land you in jail. The average cost of a sexual harassment lawsuit in 2009 was $1.8 million, and the average out-of-court settlement was $300,000. And it's really hard to operate a successful tyranny from behind bars. So, if for no other reason than to save your own skin, sexual harassment is probably not the best path for you to take.

Now several companies have entire seminars devoted to the issue of sexual harassment. New employees often have to sit through hours of lectures about the nuances of sexual harassment - what's acceptable, what's borderline, what to avoid - which I think is completely ridiculous since there's really only one rule to follow:

If you have to ask if it's OK, the answer is *NO*.

I once had to suffer through one of these seminars, such a colossal waste of time that I actually found myself counting the pores on the back of my hand – which just so you know is not how I normally spend my free time. What made it worse is that the whole thing should have taken five minutes, except every couple minutes some moron raised his hand to ask about a hypothetical scenario.

Re-Enactment of One of the Longest Days of My Life

Idiot 1: "What if my hands don't actually…"
Instructor: "No."

Idiot 2, four minutes later: "But suppose I'm just trying to give someone a compliment, and I…"
Instructor: "No."

Idiot 3, on the heels of Idiot 2: "Let's say, for argument's sake, that I barely grazed…"
Instructor: "For the last time, people, the answer is *no*."

It's not that complicated. If even a tiny portion of your minute little brain wonders if a given action will be acceptable, you're not supposed to do it. Unless you've had a 100% success rate throughout your entire life where your unsolicited groping has turned into a passionate love moment, keep your hands to yourself.[1]

Back to Work!

So, now that we've gotten *that* out of the way, let's focus on the various ways you can go about browbeating your employees.

Note: although I used the word 'browbeating,' I don't want you to stop there. Don't just beat their brows. There are plenty of other places to beat up.

Profiles in Tyranny: Bobby Knight

Easily the most controversial coach in the history of college basketball, Bobby Knight learned his inimitable style at West Point, where he coached Army for six years. It's rumored that he lobbied hard to be allowed to carry a machine gun to team practices so that he could shoot rubber riot bullets at substandard players, but all of my inquiries at the Pentagon have been met with a wall of silence.[2]

Knight became the head coach of the Indiana Hoosiers in 1971 and remained with them for over thirty years. He quickly became legendary for his constant tirades and verbal

[1] Feel free to hire me to come to your company and deliver my fully comprehensive, 4-minute seminar on sexual harassment. That's right – you too can learn how to not harass people in *only 4 minutes!!!* Visit www.jeffhavens.com to learn more!

[2] OK, I made this rumor up. But it's not entirely unbelievable, is it? And *that's* why Bobby Knight rocks!

smackdowns of players, referees, sports commentators, and pretty much everybody else who made the mistake of looking at him. But actions speak louder than words, right? So let's look at some of his coaching actions:

- In 1979, while coaching the U.S. team in the Pan American Games, Knight was arrested for striking a Puerto Rican police officer. He was convicted *in absentia* and ordered to jail for six months.
- In 1981, after an Indiana-LSU game, Knights got into an argument with an LSU fan and stuffed the kid into a trash can. Seriously.
- In 1985, Knight threw a chair onto the court while an opposing player attempted to shoot free throws.
- In 1994, Knight head-butted one of his players during a time out.
- In 1997, Knight was accused of choking one of his own players. Knight denies the charges, but videotape evidence confirms that he did.

Knight is also believed to have thrown a vase at an IU secretary's head and to have choked a random restaurant patron who complained after allegedly hearing Knight made racist comments. And in an inspired move, Knight seems also to have broken his own son's nose during a hunting trip. Thanks, Dad!

Bobby Knight's career and personal life are a valuable lesson to all aspiring tyrants. And what exactly is that lesson?

That nobody should feel safe around you. Ever. Not even your own children.

Sleep tight.

The nice thing about violence is that it actually tends to be a good motivator, at least in the short term. Sure, your employees will absolutely detest you, but they will probably do what you tell them to do in order to avoid pain. Or they'll *appear* to do what you tell them to while they secretly search for another job on company time. Either way, their resistance to your physical assault is likely to be minimal. Most people will avoid a fight at all costs, which should give you plenty of latitude to abuse them however you see fit.

And to help you get started, here are a few ideas.

New and Exciting Uses For Common Office Objects!!!

- ***Chairs*** I'm stealing a page out of Bobby Knight's playbook here. Chairs are good for two things: sitting (boring), and hurling across your office (now we're talking!). They tend to have lots of corners and make a terrific sound when they crash against things.

- ***Paperweights*** Easy to grab in a fit of rage, easy to throw, and ridiculously painful. Buy one today!

- ***Scattered papers on your desk*** In movies, the clearing of the desk is usually a prelude to one of two things: a world-class rant, or a moment of passionate and semi-spontaneous sex. Given the sexual harassment thing I mentioned earlier, I recommend you stick with the former.

- ***Filing cabinets*** Chances are you won't be able to throw this one. However, nothing can display your rage quite like the sight - and sound - of an overturned filing cabinet. You can also punch it a few times, which will add great emphasis to whatever point you're trying to make. The sight of an overturned or dented filing cabinet will teach you employees to tread lightly whenever necessity forces them to be in your presence.

- ***Computer monitors*** If you're still trapped in the 1990s and have a CRT monitor on your desk, do yourself a favor and hurl it at one of your subordinates. I mean seriously, don't you think it's time you joined the 21st century and got yourself a flatscreen?

Profiles in Tyranny – John Henry Patterson

If I've had any real difficulty throughout this book, it's been trying to pin down each *Profile in Tyranny* into a single chapter. The best tyrants do so many tyrannical things that it's hard to focus on a single theme.

Take John Henry Patterson for example. After purchasing a pair of cash registers from the National Manufacturing Company (NMC) to improve the bookkeeping for his coal supply business, Patterson and his brother bought NMC in

1884, renaming it the National Cash Register Company. The company grew, and Patterson became renowned for firing people for the most trivial reasons – for example, he fired one executive for not riding his horse properly. He also adopted the habit of repeatedly firing, re-hiring, and re-firing employees in order to break their self-esteem. He is perhaps most famous for firing Thomas Watson, who went on to become the President of IBM. I'm not sure why he fired Watson. Possibly because Watson had tied his tie improperly one day[3].

So I suppose I could focus on how he established positional dominance.

But then there's his practice of banning unhealthy foods from company premises and having all employees weighed and measured every six months. So I suppose I could focus on his ridiculously excessive micromanagement.

But then there's his conviction in 1913 of antitrust violations, which included the hiring of 'knockout men' to encourage store owners not to purchase products from NCR competitors. That little affair ended up with him and 29 other NCR executives in prison for a year. But he didn't outsource all of his violence, though, and seems to have frequently choked people, especially women. Now we know where Bobby Knight got it from!

The point, of course, is that good tyrants are multi-talented. Patterson didn't simply resort to choking his subordinates into submission. But it sure does the trick when you need to shut somebody up!

---

[3] Patterson was known to have fired at least one employee for that very reason. Seriously. *Man*, I like his style.

"Now wait a second," you might be thinking. "Sure, people used violence as a motivator back in the 1920s – they were all cavepeople back then anyway, and fascism was very popular. And it makes sense that Bobby Knight would use violence in the 1970s and 80s – after all, we were all so angry about Vietnam, and the Cold War put everybody on edge. But surely that's not a method I can get away today, is it?"

Why do you keep doubting me? I've told you before, and I'll tell you again – *every* technique in this book is market-tested. *Every* one of them has been used by managers to help create the kind of fear-based fiefdom I know you're looking to create for yourself. So if I say you can throw things and beat on people and get away with it, I mean it.

Storytime!

Seriously, do we even need another story? Of course we do! The more the merrier. And this one isn't about the president of a company or a famous basketball coach. This one involves an ordinary manager, somebody just like you!

Grace worked as a waitress at a restaurant and nightclub. Her boss had a notoriously bad temper and was well known for shouting at his employees whenever they did something to displease him. "Which was everything. I can't remember a night I worked when he didn't yell at somebody about something." But the money was good, and Grace soon got accustomed to her boss's frequent tirades. Or perhaps more accurately, she learned to deal with them because the money was good. There is a difference, you know.

But money can only carry you so far. I didn't intend that to be a pun, but it will be. Just wait.

One night, her boss was engaged in his nightly exercises at the maître'd podium; apparently one of his employees had miscounted the money in one of the restaurant's cash registers. It was an occasional problem at the restaurant, and easily fixed, but one which Grace's boss had ripped into his employees about before. On this night, though, he decided to express his anger in a new, more obvious way. Maybe he'd realized that his employees were becoming immune to his verbal assaults, or perhaps he'd recently subscribed to a UFC Pay-Per-View fight and was still on an adrenaline high. But whatever the reason, he decided to bring his point home by flinging the miscounted register drawer at Grace.

"I don't think he was aiming at me," says Grace. "I don't think he was aiming at all. I just happened to be in the right place at the right time."

It missed, thanks more to her boss's bad aim than Grace's cat-like reflexes, since she was too stunned to move. The drawer flew past her and broke against the floor a few feet behind her. There were several customers who witnessed it; some backed away, and at least one couple turned around and left. When neither Grace nor her coworkers made a move to pick up the checks, credit card slips, and cash that was now scattered across the entryway, her boss screamed at them until they did.

"He tried to buy me a drink later to apologize," Grace remembers. "I took the drink and quit the next day."

There you have it, my aspiring tyrants. As this chapter has endeavored repeatedly to point out, when words fail you, flying objects with sharp corners will not. Few things will motivate an employee like a heavy thing hurtling toward their face. Got it?

Storytime!

OK, seriously, talk about overkill. But I like this story, and I'm pretty sure you will too!

Charlie worked as part of a crew that tore down and rebuilt old bridges. He claims to have loved everything about his job except for his foreman. But when you hear about his foreman, you'll wonder how he could possibly have loved anything at all.

"My foreman absolutely hated us," Charlie says, "because his bonuses and raises were based on our performance. The company had a bonus policy for foreman and above based on safety and production. If the job was on schedule and productive and there were no injuries every month, then the bosses got bonuses. They could also opt to "let it ride" and collect a bigger bonus at the end of the job. The problem with the "let it ride" option was that it was an all-or-nothing option. If there was one bad month or one injury they lost the entire bonus for that job."

Wow. Thank you, Charlie, for sharing with the world what is quite possibly the dumbest bonus structure anybody has ever devised. So let me get this straight: your foremen were given bonuses based in part on injuries over which they couldn't possibly have any control? And since your company effectively de-monetized injuries, you're saying that any physical damage to workers was also coupled with financial damage to your bosses?

Gosh, I can't see how *that* would ever be a problem. But I'm guessing you can. Please, continue.

"So our foreman was an angry guy anyway. He was always yelling, throwing his hard hat, kicking over tool boxes and water jugs, and calling us incompetent, ignorant, slow and lazy. He even cut our lunch breaks short and had us work well into the night to keep production high and his bonus intact."

"Well, one afternoon, I stepped into a shallow uncovered manhole and injured my ankle and lower back. My boss witnessed this and came running. I thought he wanted to see if I was OK."

Oh, come on, Charlie. You know better than that, don't you?

"His first question was, 'You have health insurance, right?' I pointed out that this happened at work and that it would be considered workman's comp. He immediately got angry and told me, 'I've got my bonus built up to almost $5,000 and if you (*word I can't print!*) that up for me, I'll beat you in the parking lot with a baseball bat and show you what a real injury is!'"

That's sweet of him, isn't it? Did he bring you get-well flowers or a balloon when you were in the hospital?

"Uh, no. Fortunately this was a union job, so I was able to report him and get the help needed for my injury. He spent the following days and weeks telling me what a worthless piece of (*word I can't print!*) I was, and how I needed find a way to come up with the $5,000 I had lost him. He never did come after me with the bat, though. He was later reassigned to an office position in another location, all the while blaming me for his problems with the company."

Isn’t violence wonderful? I tell you, it was a real mistake to allow workers’ rights in this country. But fortunately, it looks like that’s about to change. Pretty soon you’ll be able to pummel your employees with impunity, just like they did when they were building the pyramids. I tell you, *those* were the good old days.

And we’re almost finished. Only one more topic to cover in order for you to be a grandmaster at trampling your underlings…then trampling them again. If you were to stop reading now, you’d be more than capable of taking what you’ve learned and becoming a perfectly onerous boss. But this last one is what really separates the tyrants from the petty thugs. It’s time to find out what you’re really made of.

Create Win/Lose Situations!

"I can hire one half of the working class
to kill the other half."
Jay Gould

And here we are, the heart of trampling your underlings, then trampling them again. I know I said earlier that there really wasn't a culminating idea to this section, but I think you were mistaken when you believed me when I said that.[1] Life is a battle, my aspiring tyrant – there are winners, and there are losers. The only way you can rise to the top is by standing on the faces of the people beneath you. You've never seen a football game where both teams won, have you?

Hmm. Actually you might have, if you live in one of those mamby-pamby communities where parents organize sporting events where they don't keep score and everybody wins because God forbid a child ever have to face the horror of losing something and damaging their oh-so-fragile self-esteem. But trust me – *trust* me – life doesn't work that way. It's kill or be killed, eat or be eaten. It's the law of the jungle, and that's what rules in the boardroom as well.

"But wait!" you might be saying. "Your football analogy is erroneous. Because it's not an individual that wins,

---

[1] Notice how I got around admitting that I was wrong? And why did I do that? *Because a tyrant is never wrong.* We'll be covering this concept more thoroughly in the next section. Stay tuned!

it's an entire team. So really, what you're saying is that in order to be successful, I need the support of my team as well. Isn't that right?"

Shut up.

Success is Failure!

If you managed to make it through 11th grade then you probably took physics. I'm sure you slept through most of it, which is why you work with people instead of lasers or telescopes or giant supercooled magnets. Physics is a discipline for people who were unable to make any friends, which is why all those scientists over in Europe are trying to create a black hole that will ultimately destroy Earth.

But it's possible that you were hopped up on caffeine and thus unable to fall asleep on the day that your physics teacher shared with you a seemingly inconsequential fact:

For every action, there is an equal and opposite reaction

It's Newton's third law of motion, and it's been verified through literally millions of experiments. You can see this principle in its most elegant incarnation if you've ever been lucky enough to witness a bar fight - for when you punch a random stranger, it's a dead certainty that he'll turn right around and punch you. It's an excellent scientific experiment, and it's really, really painful.

Anyway, the tyrant's application of Newton's Third Law is this: in an effective tyranny, every success needs to be accompanied by an equal or greater failure.

Profiles in Tyranny: Jay Gould

You know you're a tyrant when you consider *yourself* to be the most hated man in America and still keep doing what you're doing. The quintessential robber baron, Jay Gould was a railroad magnate who at his peak owned 15% of the railroad tracks in the United States, in the process making himself the 9th richest person in U.S. history. Only the ninth richest, you say? Yeah, it's unfortunate. But you can't blame him. He died from tuberculosis at 56. I'm sure if he'd had another 10 or 20 years, he'd have figured out a way to kill the eight people above him.

How did he do it? By mastering the win-lose proposition. He acquired his railroads through acquisitions, mergers, consolidations, and all the other things that businesspeople do today. But more importantly, he did it through a complete disregard of everyone else alive.

Need some examples? How about this one: in 1869 Gould began to buy gold in an effort to corner the market, hoping that an increase in the price of gold would increase the price of wheat, which would then cause wheat farmers to sell, which would then increase railroad traffic from west to east, which would then increase Gould's profits. It didn't quite work that way, though. Instead, Gould's rapid purchasing of gold caused a panic, and the price of gold plummeted 44%. Gould managed a small profit, and thousands of other people lost considerable fortunes. Sounds like a win-lose to me!

Want more? Then how about this one: in 1886 over 200,000 railroad union workers went on strike to protest low wages, unsafe working conditions, and the firing of a union official who was fired for attending a union meeting. In today's world, a strike would typically involve a lot of posturing, a lot of negotiations, and ultimately some concessions on both sides in order to achieve a mutually satisfactory end result[2]. Gould, however, had different ideas. He hired security guards to break up union meetings and physically attack union leaders; then, when that didn't crush the strike, he convinced several state governors to mobilize their state militias to confront the striking workers. Strikers retaliated by destroying railroad property and occasionally shooting at passing trains. If all this doesn't endear your workers to you, I don't know what will.

Or *this* one (this is my favorite): in 1873 Gould bribed an English noble, Lord Gordon-Gordon, with $1 million in company stock in order to secure a favorable investment from him. However, when Gordon-Gordon turned out to be a fraud, Gould sued him. Gordon-Gordon fled to Canada. So Gould had him *kidnapped.* Seriously. The kidnappers were caught, put in a Canadian prison, and refused bail, leading to an international incident in which the governor of Minnesota (one of Gould's friends and associates, by the way) mobilized thousands of Minnesota volunteers for a potential invasion of Canada.

You read that right. This dude was prepared to launch an invasion of *Canada* in order to get back at somebody who had swindled him. He would have started a war, a war with the least warlike country in the world.[3] Who would have won?

---

[2] Unless you live in Wisconsin, Indiana, or Ohio.

[3] With the possible exception of The Maldives. Seriously, nobody's ever said, "Those darned Maldivers really need to be taught a lesson."

Absolutely no one. Except Gould, of course, who would have enjoyed the sight of yet another enemy crushed underfoot.

So remember, my aspiring tyrant – when all else fails, invade Canada. Trust me, they'll never see it coming.

Title for This Section!!!

What? I couldn't think of anything clever. Get over it.

Now as with a lot of the ideas we've covered in this book, there are important distinctions to be made between normal business practices and the kinds of tyrannical win-lose scenarios that I'm hoping you'll emulate. I mean, if an invasion of Canada would help you gain an extra sliver of market share, by all means *do it*. Those self-righteous Canucks definitely need to be taken down a notch.

However, for your pedestrian situations, there are still plenty of win-lose opportunities. Offering rewards to your top-performing salesperson, as we've discussed earlier, is not a win-lose situation – at least, not necessarily. But it *can* be.

Pay Attention!!!

- ***Win/Win:*** Your sales for the year are up overall, and your top salesperson is up 25%. At your end-of-year awards banquet you reward everyone on your sales team with a bonus. Your top salesperson receives a larger bonus and is also privately asked if he/she would be willing to coach your lowest performing salesperson on sales techniques. This should help your new or inexperienced salespeople improve more rapidly while also providing your top salesperson with a management opportunity in case he/she is interested. If not, you accept that your top salesperson is happy with sales and doesn't want to manage others, then make the same request of your second-highest performing salesperson, then third-highest, and on down the line until someone accepts the challenge.

- ***Win/Not Lose***: Your sales for the year are up overall, and your top salesperson is up 25%. At your end-of-year banquet you reward your top salesperson with a bonus. Your other employees are encouraged to try harder for next year. Next year's sales quotas are based on year-over-year increase, rather than on gross revenue, in order to level the playing field and give everyone a fair shot at the top prize next year. Or you can offer two awards, one for highest sales and one for greatest year-over-year increase. Whatever – it's not like you'll be doing this anyway. *You* should do something like…

- ***Win/Lose***: Your sales for the year are up overall, and your top salesperson is up 25%. At your end-of-year banquet you reward yourself with a bonus. Your top salesperson is given a plaque or certificate of achievement. Everyone else is given higher sales quotas for next year, because next year you'd really like to give yourself a larger bonus.

That's an example for a sales department, but it's easily translatable into any department you happen to be tyrannizing. As long as victory is always accompanied by some kind of defeat, you'll be doing just fine.

And the best of you will figure out how to provide victory *and* defeat to the same person!

Storytime!

A few years ago I gave a presentation at an end-of-year awards banquet for a company that manufactures televisions and LCD screens. They loved my presentation, of course, because I'm amazing. But I'm hardly sharing this story just to toot my own horn. Not that I'd need any other reason. I'm big on horn-tooting. But I like to throw some instructional value into my stories whenever possible.

So let's double up. After my unbelievably successfully and well-received presentation, the company vice president took the stage to begin the process of handing out awards and then giving out prizes. As is common at awards banquets, each employee was given a raffle ticket, and those employees whose names were drawn received a prize. There were several prizes - $150 gift cards to various stores, electronics, trips to a local spa – and the grand prize was a 52" LCD television that at the time was probably worth a few thousand dollars.[4] Everybody was excited.

Until the vice president opened his mouth.

---

[4] That was before the prices on those things plummeted and they started giving them away with the purchase of a new house. Or they might be giving houses away with the purchase of a new TV – in today's market, either one is possible.

"All right, now before we start the prize giveaway," Mr. Vice President said (I swear I am not making any of this up), "Accounting has asked me to tell you that these prizes do count as income, so you'll have to claim the value of them on your taxes at the end of the year. Just needed to make sure you knew that. So, let's get started!"

Wow. W-O-W. I've never seen the energy of a room disappear quite that fast. Can you think of a better way to sabotage the joy of receiving a prize than by telling people it will ultimately cost them money? I sure can't. The guy who ended up winning the 52" television probably spent $600 in taxes on it. So guess what? He won *and* lost all at the same time!

Don't get me wrong – prizes are great. But they're even better when you remind people beforehand that nothing in the world is free.

Now I know this chapter has focused more on examples of win-lose behaviors than on some of the behaviors themselves. I feel like I should give you at least a few more specific ways to put the win-lose philosophy into your own personal practice.

But I'm not going to, and it has absolutely nothing to do with me having run out of things to say – trust me, I could talk forever. Just ask my friends, or the people who used to consider themselves to be my friends.

Instead, I'm just going to give you one idea. It's most commonly seen in government, but it's certainly no stranger to the private sector, and it's something I want you to absorb as fully as possible.

The Ultimate Win-Lose:
Basing Future Budgets on Previous Budgets!!!!

Every year in companies around the world, people sit down together and write up prospective budgets for their departments for the upcoming year. Each department generally tries to get a little more money for itself every year. That's understandable. But how to justify the request for a larger budget?

That's where the ultimate win-lose comes in. Because in some of these companies, future budgets are based almost entirely on past budgets. Which means that throughout the year, every department strives to spend every dollar of its allocation. Are their expenditures worth doing? WHO CARES? As long as they money gets spent, it will be easier to ask for more of it next year.

"But what about departments whose budgets have always been small but whose importance is growing faster than average?"

Well it wouldn't be the ultimate win-lose if there weren't a loser, right? And now you know who the loser is! If you haven't been receiving much money in the past, then there's no reason at all to give you any more of it in the future! Basing future budgets on past budgets is almost always predicated on the assumption that the way things have always been done is the way they need to be done in the future. Those who are currently favored with healthy budgets continue to get healthy budgets, and those without them…well, they continue to starve.

In other words: the ones in power win, while the ones without it lose. It's the perfect tyranny!

But there's more than just one loser, of course. If the company in question falls in the public sector, then it's generally taxpayers who lose, since they end up paying for things that don't need to be done. And if we're talking about the private sector, then the big loser is anything new that hasn't already become entrenched in a given company's budgeting system. Those things are generally characterized by creativity, ingenuity, and other projects that no one can guarantee will succeed – but which if they *do* succeed usually help a company prepare itself against changing conditions or branch out into emerging markets.

So really, if you put all that together, *everyone* loses!

That's a strategy you can organize yourself around. Now, let me give you a messiah to follow.

Every so often a tyrant comes along who so perfectly epitomizes the concepts I'm trying to impart that it is impossible for me to overlook their contribution to tyranny. They are true geniuses, masters of their chosen field, the way Degas was a master at painting and that silver dude in Times Square is a master at getting paid to do nothing. And when I am confronted with such a paragon of perfection, I can do little but nod respectfully in their direction, share with you their shining example, and hope that some of their wisdom trickles down into your small but developing brain.

Profiles in Tyranny: Donald Trump

Donald Trump is one of the most well-recognized businesspeople in the world. So well recognized, in fact, that in a recent poll 28% of Americans said they think he would make an ideal boss – a statistic which, if true, provides irrefutable evidence for the argument that America is one of the most poorly educated industrialized countries in the world.

So, what makes Donald Trump a tyrant? It's not the combover, which has done much to bring awareness to combover victims across the world.[5] It's not his beautiful daughter Ivanka, whose demeanor is so cold and unloving that she might actually be a robot. Rather, it's his flagship creation, NBC's *The Apprentice*, which makes Mr. Trump our best example for this section.

The Apprentice has now just ended its 10th season. A full decade. And thank God for it. Because what a fantastic role model for America! I can hear him pitching it to the network executives now.

"I have an idea, everybody. What if – hear me out here – what if we create a show where teams of employees compete not only with other teams, which would approximate the normal workings of global business, but also compete with the members of their *own* team. That way – you following me? – all 'employees' will simultaneously be trying to succeed while also attempting to sabotage the members of their own group,

[5] It would not surprise me to learn that Donald Trump has attempted to patent the combover. Nor would it surprise me to learn that he's attempted to patent hair.

whose efforts they need to exploit in order to succeed by the way. Then, at the end, when one team has vanquished the other, we can enjoy the process of watching the members of the losing team tear each other to pieces as they attempt to save themselves from a man – that'd be me – whose most famous saying is, 'You're fired.'"

This in one of the worst economies America has faced in 75 years. And now the man who got famous by firing people is reputed to be seriously considering a bid for the presidency. Can't wait to see *his* jobs initiative![6]

Thank you, Donald. I could not have done it better myself.

So if things in your department or company seem to be running just a little bit too smoothly, it might be time to take a page out of Mr. Trump's playbook. He'll probably sue you for it if he ever finds out, since I'm sure he's copyrighted competition and teams and business and verbs and cauliflower and just about everything else. But until then, his is an unparalleled model for creating the kind of win-lose situations that ensure your employees a) never get anything useful done, and b) hate themselves and everyone else while they do it. Enjoy!

At this point you should be pretty proud of yourself. Your tyranny is humming along. Your position is secure, the

---

[6] He bailed out. A couple weeks ago, he tipped his hand and let the whole world know that he was just using the presidency as a giant marketing ploy. There will come a day when *Who Wants to Be The President?* becomes a hit reality show. It's coming, people. Repent while there's time.

people beneath you are cowed and unhappy, and things look like they'll continue this way forever.

But don't get too comfortable. Problems are always just around the corner, waiting for you to let your guard down so they can sneak up and strike you unawares. We've covered how to deal with your environment and your employees, but we haven't really talked about what to do in the inevitable event that things don't end up going exactly according to your master plan.

And yet, your Sherlock-Holmes-like sleuthing skills have probably helped you realize that this book is only about halfway done. Mayhap there are still some goodies left?

Mayhap there are. Turn the page. Or better yet, have one of your employees do it for you!

Outsource Blame!

Outsource Blame!

"The search for someone to blame
is always successful."
Robert Half

"It's not whether you win or lose,
it's how you place the blame."
Oscar Wilde

By now you have effectively crushed your employees' will to produce. It's time now to transition into the gentle art of Outsourcing Blame.

Outsourcing, as I'm sure you know, is the most popular business model of the recent past, immediate present, and foreseeable future. In the last 20 years U.S. corporations have outsourced hundreds of thousands of textile, manufacturing, customer service, technology, and all manner of other jobs. Indians with names like Rajeevalochana christen themselves 'David' and pretend to answer your tech support questions from an office in Maryland; companies ship materials to China and ship finished products back for a fraction of the cost of building those products at home. Given outsourcing's wild success in the past few decades, it's predicted that in the next five years American companies will also begin to outsource water, oxygen, complex thought, and the entire American middle class.

So, since outsourcing is the wave of the business future, it makes sense that you should want to outsource blame as well. Because from time to time, mistakes will happen. Things will go wrong. The strongest walls occasionally crack; the most unsinkable ship occasionally runs into the unexpected iceberg; and (my personal favorite here) an undefeated football team occasionally loses the Super Bowl.

Several studies have shown that the early admission of a mistake will engender more loyalty and goodwill than if the mistake had not been made in the first place

Ignore that last thing. I tried to delete it a thousand times, but it just kept coming back. Something must be wrong with my computer.

Anyway, it should go without saying that a tyrant *does not make mistakes.* His or her subordinates make mistakes. They are flawed, imperfect, barely worth the air they breathe, which of course is why you need to remain a tyrant; if you didn't maintain your iron grip on power, the idiots you employ would bring everything to a screeching halt.

There are two reasons that it's so important for you to outsource blame. The first, which we've alluded to, is that it's important (and don't forget enjoyable!) to whitewash your failures by attributing them to others. But you also need to keep in mind the tyrants who have come before you. I can think of no examples of tyrants ever blaming themselves for the failings of their regimes. Hitler certainly didn't blame himself for the complete destruction he brought upon Germany, and there are plenty of business leaders who have adopted his approach.

Profile in Tyranny: Alan Schwartz

Alan Schwartz, the former CEO of Bear Stearns, is perhaps known for overseeing the catastrophic disintegration of a multi-billion dollar company during the subprime debacle of 2007. How catastrophic? Well, Bear Stearns watched its share price plunge from $133.20 to under $10 in less than a year, and the company was eventually swallowed by JP Morgan Chase, which stopped using the Bear Stearns name in 2010. The company vanished. However, it has been documented in a handful of fuzzy photographs and is believed to reside now in the same stretches of uninhabited countryside where Bigfoot makes his woodland home.

However, to tyrants around the world, Schwartz is even better known for the way he avoided any sense of personal responsibility for his company's destruction.

They always say that actions speak louder than words, but some words are really, *really* loud. Like these words, which Alan Schwartz actually said in an interview with the New York Times:

"Looking backwards, if I'd have known exactly the forces that were coming, what actions could we have taken to

have avoided this situation? I simply have not been able to come up with anything that would have made a difference."

Me either, Alan! I have been racking my brains, trying to figure out what an investment company could possibly have done to avoid getting caught up in the subprime mortgage crisis. I'm sure there was absolutely no way you could have identified the crisis before it began (like Goldman Sachs) and pulled out of subprime investments. I'm sure your company's decision to *increase its exposure* to the subprime market by buying more of those securities in 2006 and 2007 was inevitable. I'm sure there was absolutely no way to prevent Bear Stearns from becoming so highly leveraged – 35-to-1, by one reckoning – that any negative movement in the markets would have been swift and severe. You're right! Failure and collapse were unavoidable. You did the best you could.

I wish I were your son. Not only because I'd probably be driving a nicer car than I currently am, but also because I wouldn't have had to listen to any of that tedious "Try Harder" crap that my parents gave me whenever I ran into an obstacle. Study for my tests? Are you kidding me? What's the point?

Ok I'm done now.

So if you hope to become as misguided and despotic as these people, you'll need to learn to blame others for everything that goes wrong on your watch.

Ha. 'Learn to.' As though you don't already know how!

The Undisputed Masters

I know I just gave you an example of a business leader outsourcing blame, and he did a great job. Why? Because instead of outsourcing it to a particular person, *he outsourced it to forces entirely beyond human control.* It's an excellent technique, as it diffuses blame over such a large area that it's hard for anyone to figure out where the problem started.

But it's not as tyrannical as it should be. If you'll remember the chapter on creating win-lose situations, you'll know that in the tyrant's ideal world, there should be always be a loser.

And nobody is better at placing blame on other people quite like…

Profiles in Tyranny: Congress!

Wow. What more can I say? These people are *amazing!* They are the undisputed masters of outsourcing blame, and the ones that I want you to always have in mind when you're perfecting this technique.

Congress has been blaming others for their failures for as long as there has been a Congress. The First Continental Congress, in fact, tasked George Washington and other Revolutionary generals with the seemingly impossible assignment of waging a war against Britain without providing those generals with any way to pay their soldiers. How is that, exactly? Because that Congress didn't have the authority to levy taxes.

I'm going to repeat that. Our country's first Congress did not have the ability to levy taxes. Man, *those* were the days!

But I'm straying from the point, which is that our Congress is better than any other organization on our planet at finding scapegoats for their failings. Let's take the current recession, which began in 2007 and which will hopefully end before the world blows up. Whose fault is it? I'll tell you whose fault it is: ***not theirs!!!***

Let's see...who has Congress attempted to throw under the bus...

- Republicans!
- Democrats!
- Obama!
- Bush!
- Clinton!
- FDR![1]
- Timothy Geithner!
- Henry Paulson!
- Ben Bernacke!
- Alan Greenspan!
- Insurance companies!
- Illegal immigrants!
- China!
- The banking industry!
- Wall Street!
- Irresponsible homeowners!

[1] Seriously, I've heard at least Congressperson blame Roosevelt for a 21st-century financial crisis. Good choice – he can't even fight back!

- Saudi Arabia!
- Satan!
- Snuffleupagus!

OK, so I made that last one up. But in general, Congress has blamed anybody and everybody but themselves. I have not heard one Congressmen take any portion of the responsibility for our current economic situation. Not *one* of them has admitted to having helped pass and repeal laws that collectively deregulated the financial services industry and encouraged our financial institutions to take unhealthy risks. You will never be better at outsourcing blame than Congress. All you can hope to do is come close.

You Can Do It!

Now I know I've just given you an example that you can never hope to match. But I don't want you to lose heart. Outsourcing blame happens to be the easiest section in the entire *Unleash Your Inner Tyrant!* program. This is something you have known how to do from birth. It's as easy as learning to speak or learning to breathe.

And I'll prove it to you.

I want you to find a group of your coworkers. You can do this exercise at lunch, in the breakroom, or really anywhere that you and a handful of people are congregating. I want you to ask them all to imagine that you are working on a joint project, and that something has gone wrong. Then, without allowing for any discussion or thoughtful analysis, I want you all to decide which person in your group is going to be blamed by everybody else. Each person should point his or her finger at one of your group members, and you should give them no more than five seconds to decide.

I hope you try this exercise for yourself, but in case you don't, let me tell you what will happen. Without thinking, without any communication of any kind, the group will *automatically* decide to blame the same person. It won't be you, because you are leading the exercise. It will be somebody else. Somehow, everyone in the group will instinctively know the weakest among you, and they'll descend like vultures. It's a beautiful thing to see.

It also illustrates an important axiom of outsourcing blame, one that I've phrased as a rhyme to help you more easily remember it:

Don't linger, point the finger!

Fair warning: you can point whichever finger you want, but there's one of them that will get you sent straight to HR.

Also, an important note: there are two different ways that the person being blamed might react. He or she might fight back. They might stand defiant, finger outstretched, daring you to toss him or her to the wolves. And you should appreciate their spirit and fire - *because it's useless!* It's adorable to watch the condemned try to proclaim their innocence. If several people are blaming him or her, then all the proclamations in the world won't do a bit of good. It's a democracy, which means somebody has to lose.

But there's another way they might react, which is to quietly *accept* the blame. They'll see the writing on the wall;

they'll know that resistance is futile. And so instead of fighting a losing battle, they'll take whatever the world throws at them. *THIS IS EXACTLY WHAT WE WANT!!!!* Because once you've broken a person that far, you can subsequently blame them for *everything* that goes wrong.

Seriously, try this exercise for yourself. I do it at my corporate presentations, and it never fails to bring a smile to people's faces. Except the people being blamed, of course, but we don't need to care about them.

Encourage Alliances and Engage in Factional Warfare!

If you've paid attention throughout your life, you should already know that it's significantly easier to blame others when you have some help. If you're blaming somebody and they're blaming you, the issue devolves into a he-said/she-said affair that makes it difficult to know the outcome. Sometimes the world will blame your antagonist, and somebody they'll blame you. And we can't have that. A tyrant knows how to create better odds than that.

Fortunately, the more people you have on your team, the more obvious the outcome. If one finger is pointing at your chosen scapegoat, they might survive; but if four, or seven, or thirty-two fingers are pointing at that same person, the end result is much easier to predict. Which is why you should encourage alliances and engage in factional warfare. Obviously these alliances will be temporary, as you will eventually be forced to turn on everyone who helped you rise to power. Perhaps now it's making a little more sense why I used the example of Donald Trump in the previous section.

So, how does this work? Well, because you're dumb, and because I'm an awesome teacher, I'll show you.

Factional Warfare Time!

Scenario 1 – Scattershot Approach: You work in a marketing department, and your company is rolling out a new product. Because you are uncertain if the product is going to sell as much as your company is hoping it will, and because you know that you're likely to be blamed for doing a poor job of successfully marketing the product to potential buyers, you initiate a series of conversations with your superiors about problems you've been having with your company's R&D, Design, and Sales departments regarding the new product rollout. Then, if sales do indeed fail to meet projections, you can refer back to those conversations as evidence of everyone else's guilt! If only people had listened to you sooner, things would have been so much better!

Scenario 2 – The Double-Edged Sword: You and two others – for the sake of simplicity, let's call them Worker Bee and Corporate Drone – are working on a project. It is clear that Corporate Drone is not pulling his weight. You and Worker Bee agree to mention Corporate Drone's inadequate work when you're asked to provide a performance review. However, when the performance review comes, you slander Worker Bee instead, because you know that she is going to complain about Corporate Drone. That way you'll look like the best of the lot!

Scenario 3 – The Flailing Walrus: You're the lowest performing member of your sales team. Everyone knows it, and anyway the numbers don't lie. When it's time to dialogue with your boss about how things could be improved, you accuse everyone else of working in concert to bring you down. One coworker stole your clients; another co-opted your computer; a third failed to answer your questions about the new software like he said he would; still another gave you bad sales advice. It won't work, and it will definitely alienate you from everyone in your office. But sometimes being a tyrant isn't about being a winner. Sometimes it's just about being a jerk.

Scenario 4 – The Blame Professional: Do you remember back in college when you were asked to do a group assignment? You know how those always turned out – one or two overachievers did all the work and the rest of you screwed off, eating pizza and promising to do work that you had no intention of doing. It's a habit you've carried into your professional life, although you're well aware that it's an impossible one to maintain without others catching on. So, in order to save yourself, you spend your entire working day criticizing others' work, finding fault with others' methods, and generally sending a barrage of emails to your superiors about the inferior abilities of your teammates. This operation requires your full attention, which means that you're spending 20-40 hours a week on it. It's a lot of work for somebody who doesn't want to work, and it's rather strange that you're willing to spend so much time finding fault with others when you could be spending that time contributing in a positive manner. You might even have trouble taking a vacation because you know that your coworkers will turn on you in your absence. But as I've said before, tyranny has very little to do with logic.

There are other scenarios that I had fully intended to share with you. I'd planned this chapter to be much longer, more comprehensive, and more informative than it is. But my editors decided that it needed to be a certain length, so there you have it. Seriously, I'm not stopping here because I'm lazy and don't feel like writing anymore. It's my editors. Those people have no idea what they're doing. I don't even know how they got their jobs. You've probably caught a couple misspellings in this book already, haven't you? I'm telling you, there's a reason that *editor* and *rodent* share a lot of the same letters.

Oh, and don't even get me *started* on my publicists. Given that this is inexplicably not the most popular book in the world, it seems pretty obvious that a trained monkey could have done a better job.

Hoard Credit!!!

"A good leader takes
a little more than his share of the blame,
a little less than his share of the credit."
Arnold H. Glasgow

Have you ever heard of Arnold H. Glasgow? Me either. I found this quote during a random Google search, and it was so astonishingly horrible that I felt compelled to put it in here. Do you see what happens when you say stupid things like this, Arnold? Do you see what happens? You die in obscurity, that's what happens.

So, let's get to it. The flip side of outsourcing blame, the *yin* to its tyrannical *yang,* is hoarding credit. Receiving recognition for good work is consistently among the top ten most important elements in employee job satisfaction surveys - and if you eliminate all financial considerations, it's consistently second in importance, right behind "opportunities for advancement." So if you want to crush those in your path, it's important that you ascribe every success to your efforts and your efforts alone.

Is it true that you couldn't have done it without your team? Yes. But more importantly for the purposes of this book, *your team couldn't have done it without you*!

An Ernst & Young survey conducted in February 2003 concluded that a majority of respondents from the U.S. and Britain believed that nonfinancial performance constitutes 40% or more of the value of any enterprise.

Can you believe that? Forty percent of the perceived value of a company, or a job, is rooted in intangible rewards. Chief among those intangible rewards is the sense of pride and self-worth that comes when you receive credit for a job well done. And if you put this all together, what it really means is that by hoarding credit, *you can increase your own job satisfaction by up to 40%!!!*

Who wouldn't want to feel 40% better about their job? I certainly would. In fact, I can't think of a single thing on Earth that I wouldn't prefer to have 40% more of. I'd love to have 40% more power, 40% more Gulfstream jets[1], 40% more friends, 40% *better* friends - the list goes on and on and on. And if I can feel 40% better about my job by taking all the credit I can find, then I see no reason not to.

What's more, there an advantage that comes from receiving credit. Several advantages, actually.

---

[1] Which unfortunately for me would still leave me with zero Gulfstream jets. But maybe a 40% boost would get me a subscription to *Gulfstream Jet Owners Monthly*, and then I could casually toss it on a coffee table in my office. Then, when people came by they'd see it and say, "You have a Gulfstream jet?" And I'd say, "What? Oh, that. Yeah I do. It's just a Gulfstream 4 – I think the newer ones are a bit pretentious – but it's still nothing to complain about. It's being maintenanced this week." And then I'd probably get a few more dates. 40% more, to be exact.

Individuals who regularly receive recognition and praise tend to increase their productivity and engagement, are more likely to stay with an organization, receive higher loyalty and satisfaction scores from customers, and have better safety records and fewer accidents

"But wait!" you might be thinking. "Wouldn't my employees like to feel 40% better about their jobs, too? Don't they deserve – "

Just stop. Stop right there. Don't even finish that sentence.

Your employees are *expendable.* They always have been, but never more so than right now, on the heels of a difficult recession and a stubbornly high unemployment rate. We're floating near 9-10% unemployment. You know what that means? *It means that you can replace your employees as many times as you want!!!* There will always be somebody eager to take the job that your dissatisfied, under-recognized former employees are running away from.

"Yeah, I know, but training new employees all the time seems prohibitively expensive and time-consuming. It just seems like it would make more sense to make the ones I have happy so that they stay longer, work harder, and produce more."

Seriously, you're making my head hurt.

Those Who Don't Know History...

I know what you're read before. I've read the same poisonous books, and I consider myself lucky to have avoided contracting the disease that they're trying to infect the entire world with. I'm sure you've been told that praise is a gift that increases as you give it away, a blessing that costs nothing and repays a thousand times over.

And if that's what you think, then you simply don't know history. Because the history of our species is one in which credit is constantly being ascribed to individuals over groups. Read enough history, and you'll learn the truth. Teams accomplish nothing. Single men and women do.

Don't believe me? OK, who was responsible for our victory in the Revolutionary War? I'll tell you who: George Washington. He freed us from the British yoke. Not Horatio Gates, the general who led the Continental Army to victory in the Battle of Saratoga; not the soldiers themselves, who actually did all of the fighting; not the French, without whose assistance the final victory over Cornwallis at Yorktown would have been impossible; not the tens of thousands of revolutionary sympathizers who provided food, shelter, equipment, and moral support to the exhausted Revolutionary armies - George Washington did it. He did it entirely by himself. Most people know that Washington had wooden teeth, but do you know why? It's because his original teeth were eventually worn down to nubs from all the bullets that he caught in his mouth and crushed into powder as he was advancing alone on the ranks of British redcoats across all 13 colonies.

And the same is true everywhere you look throughout human history. Genghis Khan rode unaccompanied across the steppes of central Asia and inflicted terror and domination wherever he went. Julius Caesar conquered Gaul with nothing more than a sword and a well-worn leather jerkin.

Mark Zuckerberg built Facebook into a billion-dollar business without any programming help or outside investment or anything but his own brain and a metric ton of caffeine. Steve Jobs actually builds every Apple computer himself, mining the silicon himself and then painstakingly soldering all the circuits using a secret machine he created from a spaceship that crash-landed near his home when he was a boy.

At least, that's how history will remember it. And what really matters? The way people feel now, or the way people in the future will look back at your legacy? Who's more important to you – the people you surround yourself with every day, or people you'll never meet who will take a collection of scattered facts and use those to piece together a rough approximation of the person you were?

So stop fighting! Give in to the inevitable. If you stretch the timeline out far enough, credit always gets concentrated into a single person. And the sooner you accept that fact, the happier and more tyrannical you'll be.

Déjà vu Time!

And the example I want you to keep in mind here?

Profiles in Tyranny: Congress!

Mwah ha!

Saw that coming from a mile away, didn't you? Of *course* you did – and if you didn't, I know you'll convince yourself that you did. You sure should have. These people are just the best role models in the world!

I'm not even going to bother with providing examples of this. I don't need to. It's too easy, like shooting fish in a barrel. You don't need an example for this concept.

Why? *Because everybody knows how to take undue credit!!!*

Storytime!

Jane was a project manager for a production company. She was accustomed to working with multiple vendors, budgets, and deadlines in order to satisfy several parties at once. And all she asked for was a little thanks now and then for a job well done. That shouldn't be too hard to give, should it?

But of course, you know the answer to that. Let's watch her fall out of love with her job, shall we?

"My department Director asked me and a co-worker to create a high-quality brochure to showcase the department's expertise as a production company with a focus on our technological expertise and experienced personnel," Jane says. "My co-worker and I conducted research, interviewed and employed a copywriter and graphics designer, put bids out for a printer, rummaged through over 5,000 photos to pick the best of the best, etc. Our main goal was not only to produce a top-notch project, but also to stay under budget."

Well, all of that sounds normal, right? I don't see any problems yet. What's the –

"The wind was quickly taken out of our sails because each step of the way required our Director's approval on every little revision of a word, comma, semi-colon or movement of a photo. My co-worker and I were exhausted by the constant double clutching – it was always hurry up and go, then screech to a halt. After months and months *and months*, we finally got the piece to the printer and were shown a final proof before thousands of copies of this brochure were to be printed. Typically, at the final proof stage, you are allowed to make revisions on your behalf, but it costs a nice chunk of change. Well, after SEVEN nice chunks of change (or proofs) by the Director, our budget was completely blown out of the water and the printer's patience was microchip thin. They were about ready to fire us as a client!"

Classic micromanagement. We've already covered that, Jane. Where's the taking credit for all your hard work? Why did I bother to include this story in this chapter if you're not going to –

"FINALLY the glorious day came when the 16-page brochure was delivered to our doorstep. (From start to finish, what should have taken four to five months ended up taking over a year to produce!) Our Director was very proud of the piece; he showed it off to his superiors and received numerous accolades. And not once did I or my co-worker ever hear directly from him. Not one thank you, not one appreciative murmur about our efforts, or our endurance in sticking with this project, or all the skillful negotiating we had to do to keep the copywriter, graphics designer and printer from lynching us at various points during the progression of this project."

That's what I'm talking about!!!! There we go – finally, the credit-hoarding I've been waiting for!

"Oh, I'm not finished. The Director was so proud of this piece, in fact, that he asked us to enter it in a prestigious advertising/marketing competition, where it earned an award placement in the category of distinguished brochures produced for the year. We attended the awards ceremony, along with our Director and several others from our department. And just before the awards began, with all of our peers in attendance, guess who told us he was going to accept the award on behalf of the department?!?!!"

Oh! Oh! Pick me! I know the answer! I know!

"Our Director beamed with such glory in his acceptance speech as he stood up there alone on stage. And surprise surprise! Guess which two peons were not given recognition as contributors to this project?"

You and your co-worker! You got no credit at all, right? That's my final answer, and I'm locking it in!

"We were thunderstruck. That's the only word for it. In fact, every time I hear AC/DC's "Thunderstruck," the whole incident comes flooding back. Because that's exactly what he did. He stole our thunder."

Congratulations, AC/DC Tyrant! All around you, employees are seething at your blatant disregard for their efforts. They truly hate you. And the best part is, you're too oblivious to notice! You are so uninterested in their feelings that you probably don't even realize they have any. With any good luck you'll make it through your entire career without catching on. In fact, if you play your cards right, the only moment of thoughtful self-reflection you should have in your entire professional life will come right at the end of it, when you can't quite figure out why everyone who works for you is so effusive in their applause at your retirement party.

But that day's a long way off. So take what you can while you can! The tyrant's life is yours!

And you can do this to. Taking undue credit is the easiest thing in the entire world, and I'll prove it.

You remember last chapter, when I asked you to form a group and then find a scapegoat to blame for your hypothetical problem? Well, I want you to do the same thing again - only *this* time, instead of pointing your finger at the worst person in your group, I want you to point at the *best* person.

I'll give you three seconds.

…

…

…

Time's up. And I already know what happened. You didn't agree, did you? You didn't easily and instinctively decide which person to point at. The vast majority of you pointed at yourselves and pretended to laugh in a facsimile of camaraderie when others in your group did the same. You'll never agree, because it's impossible. And that's exactly the way it should be – at least for you.

Storytime!

Executive at a Company I Gave a Presentation To: So, that should do it for all the five-year awards, now for the ten…(pauses as someone whispers in his ear)…wait, did I miss somebody? Sarah? Sarah who? She's not on the list. Oh, well, come on up, Sarah, we don't have a certificate for you but we'll get that taken care of for you this week, OK?[2]

[2] True story.

Storytime Again!

Announcer: And the award for Best Actor goes to....Jeff Havens! (wild applause)

Me: Thank you. Wow. This is quite an honor. I'd like to thank...um...*me*, I guess. I'm pretty sure I wouldn't have won this award without me, and all the amazing things I do. I am the best actor this year, and this award merely confirms what I've always known. I'm going to go backstage now and look at myself in a mirror for a few hours.[3]

Congratulations are Probably in Order!!!!

Do you remember way back in *Remain Aloof and Above!* when I told you that you were probably already very good at avoiding contact with your employees? If you'll remember, the average time managers spend discussing work with their employees is approximately 4 hours per employee per year. It was my way of letting you know that you were probably already following my advice, and I was so proud of you I would have placed your picture on my mantle if I had a picture of you. Or a mantle.

Well, I'm about to prematurely congratulate you again. Because I'm guessing that you've accidentally stumbled onto this piece of wisdom. Chances are that you're already very good at hoarding credit. How do I know that? Because of this statistic:

---

[3] This, too, will be a true story someday. Oh yes.

One poll found that as astounding 65% of Americans reported receiving no recognition for good work in the past year

Sixty-five percent! That's freaking amazing! Well over half of your employees either do not receive praise for the good things that they do, or don't *feel* like they receive any praise, which is essentially the same thing. But all that missing praise has to be ending up somewhere, right? It can't just evaporate into the atmosphere. So odds are, it's ending up right on your shoulders. Congratulations!

There are precious few things you can do more effectively as a tyrant than to reduce the reward of working down to nothing more than a paycheck. Unfortunately you can't take that away, thanks to a bunch of stupid laws that got passed around 1865. However, a paycheck is something that the average employee can get pretty much anywhere. More importantly, most employees are aware of that fact. So as long as the only 'reward' your employees are receiving is a purely financial one, you should ensure that they only stay indentured to you long enough to find another job with another paycheck and the potential for other, intangible rewards. And in case I haven't said this often enough, a successful tyrant doesn't let *anyone* stick around long enough to become skilled or popular, since either would be a threat to your unquestioned supremacy.

Well, I feel good about what we've accomplished here. You've learned how to take credit for other people's successes, as well as how to blame them for your failures. It's pretty straightforward. And you've done such a good job that I think it's time for a treat. Turn the page, my aspiring tyrant - there might not be an ice cream cone waiting for you, but I promise it's just as deliciously sinful.

Bonus section time!!!

Sucking Like a Champion!

Charging People for Things They're Used to Getting for Free!!!

Hello, and welcome to another installment of *Sucking Like a Champion!* We're going to take a little departure in this section from our normal regimen. Up until now we've focused on unleashing your inner tyrant on your employees and other co-workers. And we'll continue to focus on that for the rest of the book as well. But I feel like this book would be incomplete if I didn't offer you at least one way to tyrannize your customers as well. After all, those people shouldn't be immune from your barbarism, should they?

The very word *customer,* in fact, is an indication of the abysmal esteem in which you should regard them. It is derived from the Persian word *khoostaum,* which loosely translates to 'spawn of the devil camel.'[1] And if you've ever seen a gaggle of customers crowded around a clothing rack at Christmastime, I think you'd agree that it's a very accurate description indeed.[2]

---

[1] Look it up if you don't believe me.

[2] OK I was kidding. Don't look it up.

And so right now we're going to focus on a relatively new phenomenon in the world of customer service: charging people for things they used to get for free. As a regular customer myself, I can tell you from personal experience that nothing, absolutely *nothing*, will make your customers despise you quite like this technique. Remember it, use it, and watch the magic happen.

There are a million examples I could use here, but the two most impressive examples I can think of are the airline and hotel industries. Is anyone shocked that these are the two examples I came up with? I didn't think so.

Allow me to put you into the minds of some of the most effective customer service tyrants the world has ever known...

Airline tyrant: "So wait a second. You're saying we could make $34 billion a year by charging people to check their luggage? And we've just been *including* that in the price of their ticket this whole time? What are we waiting for? Our customer satisfaction ratings are already in the toilet, it's not like this will push them any lower. Plus we'll get to watch everyone try to cram gigantic suitcases into the overhead bins in a maddening and often useless attempt to avoid paying the new fees. But wait, Spirit Airlines is now going to charge people to store carry-on luggage too? This is brilliant! Let's see, what else can we charge them for that we used to just give away....what about charging them for food? Perfect! And headsets? Excellent! What about using the bathroom? You're kidding – RyanAir is already talking about that? This is fantastic, how did we not think of this before? Can we charge them for their seats? ... Oh, you're saying that's what their ticket actually pays for, huh? Well, what if we charge them extra to put their feet on the floor, or to *recline* their seats? What if we charge them *to go through security!!!* I'm telling you, the possibilities are endless here."

Hotel tyrant: "Listen, all I'm saying is that just because our guests pay $249 a night to stay here doesn't mean they should expect anything more than a bed and maybe a hot shower...No, there's absolutely no reason for anybody to expect the Internet to be included in the price of their room...Yes, I know the Internet hasn't been a luxury since 1994...Yes, I know that anybody who's paying $249 a night for a hotel room uses the Internet as an integral part of their business...Yes, I know they can over to Denny's and get wireless access for the price of a waffle...No, you're not listening, I don't *care* that every budget hotel in the world offers free wireless service as an amenity. We're not a budget hotel, we don't *have* to offer amenities. It's a privilege just to be in this building, how are you not getting this?"[3]

[3] Seriously, luxury hotel people – have you *ever* done a customer survey on this? Because I have. And take my word for it, there isn't a single person who doesn't complain about it. Not one. Anywhere. In the world.

So there you have it, my aspiring tyrant. Charge your customers for things they used to get for free, and you'll ensure that a healthy percentage of them never darken your doorstep again. And seriously, why would you want them to?

When in Doubt….Lie!

"No man has a good enough memory
to make a successful liar."
Abraham Lincoln

"With lies you may get ahead in the world,
but you can never go back."
Russian proverb

The opening quotes for this chapter illustrate two very important points.

First, it's pretty obvious that Abraham Lincoln would never get elected President today. With a nickname like "Honest Abe," he'd be laughed right out of contention.

Second, it's equally obvious that Russia lost the Cold War. And do you know why? Because of idiotic proverbs like that one, which weakened the minds of the Russian people just enough to allow America to beat them into blubbering submission.

93% of managers do not rank their leaders' communication as totally truthful

Make no mistake – lying is one of the most effective ways for tyrants to deal with problems. From time immemorial, lies have been the cornerstone on which all tyrannies are established and maintained.

Lying: A Brief History

In the beginning, there was the sun. Then the Earth was made out of rocks and water and air and magma and stuff. Then people came along. Then, four minutes after that, lies were invented.

History lesson over.

There are two major reasons that you'll need to get into the habit of lying your head[1] off. The first - and most important - reason is that there will occasionally be times when problems come upon you so swiftly and unexpectedly that it will be impossible to blame others for them. In a perfect world there would be a ready scapegoat for everything that happens, but reality is unfortunately a little less kind. Every so often, your *only* option to avoid responsibility for mistakes and failures will be to lie your way out of them.

The second - and most enjoyable - reason to lie is a bit more nuanced and is best expressed through a cute story.

Do you remember when you were a child - maybe four, possibly seven - and Christmas was just around the corner? It had always been your favorite holiday, a time filled with electricity and expectation and the thrill of infinite possibility.

---

[1] Not the word I wanted to use, but this is a family book, so.

But this particular year there was something slightly amiss. Your enthusiasm had hairline cracks in it this year, because you'd recently heard a vicious rumor: that Santa Claus wasn't real. You'd tried to brush it off, and your parents had reassured you over and over again that the kids at your elementary school didn't know what they were talking about. You'd allowed yourself to be persuaded, because you wanted to believe. But slowly and inexorably it had become more and more difficult for you to do so. Now that you thought about it, how did *one* person visit everyone on Earth in a single night? Was Santa's sleigh the size of a cruise ship? It would have to be, wouldn't it, for hundreds of millions of toys to fit? And just how *big* was Santa, anyway? I mean, you knew that cookies were delicious, but even *you* couldn't imagine knocking back a few million of them in an 8-hour stretch. Santa must weigh 1,000 pounds and have no teeth left, which wasn't at all how you'd pictured him all these years.

You held onto your belief through the holiday – mostly because you were afraid your doubts, if voiced, would deny you the special Santa present you'd been praying for since October. But shortly after, when the fever pitch had died down a little, you sat down with your parents and uttered those fateful words:

"Santa's not real, is he?"

Your parents looked at you for a moment. The silence stretched. And then: "No, sweetheart. He isn't."

And your world crumbled around you. It wasn't real. This beautiful, perfect world you'd been living in your entire life was suddenly exposed as a cheap and tawdry lie, a convenient fiction your parents had used to laugh at your expense. You probably cried a little, partially at the loss of

Santa Claus but mostly because you now knew, with dreadful certainty, that you would never be able to trust anything your parents told you again.

That's why you need to lie. Because creating that feeling in your employees is one of the finer pleasures in this world, and I'd hate for you to be deprived of it.

Alternatives to Lying – As If You Really Need Any!

Now I know that it's possible that you're a milksop, a mamby-pamby Momma's boy who doesn't want to lie because some during your sorry childhood some misguided role model told you that lying was bad. Have you forgotten how they lied to you about Santa Claus, *and* the Easter Bunny, *and* the Tooth Fairy, *and* all those times they told you that your junior high outfits and hairstyles were cool?

However, in the interest of giving you as comprehensive a guide to tyranny as possible, I've included a small number of non-lying ways to avoid responsibility for your failures and mistakes.

Ways to Deal with Problems!

- **Wait for them to blow over** Problems? What problems? I don't see any problems.

- **Focus on a different area** Your marketing efforts are a complete failure? Sounds like the *perfect* time to pour all your energy into R&D then, doesn't it! I'm sure the marketing stuff will sort itself out. Things have a way of taking care of themselves.

- **'Decide' that whatever you were doing wasn't the right direction to be going in the first place**
  You don't blame scientists for abandoning a line of research once they've decided it isn't fruitful, do you? Of course not. So why would anybody blame you for taking things in a different direction if you've decided that your original path wasn't the best one? ... What's that? You only made that decision after several other people told you that you were careening down a dangerous road? No, I don't think that's how it really happened. Sorry – you're remembering things wrong.

There are more strategies, of course, but I feel like I've teased you long enough. I've been on plenty of dates, and I know that eventually we need to get past the small talk.

Enough of That Crap – Let's Get To It!

Any of the above methods will work. They also have the advantage of being extremely popular. And yet, none of them can deliver the same sweet, seductive satisfaction that a good straight-faced lie can. None of them can make you feel like you've gotten away with something you have no business getting away with.

The art of lying is actually rather simple. In fact, after interviewing thousands of people, reading hundreds of books, observing people for dozens of years, and telling two or three amazing lies myself, I've distilled the art of lying into a remarkably simple two-step process that should have you lying in no time at all.

How to Lie in Two Easy Steps!

- Open your mouth
- Start talking

That's it. I'm not going to sit here and waste my life trying to explain the art of lying to you, because I know you've been doing it for as long as you've been alive. It's bred into our DNA, and anybody who says otherwise has quite obviously never watched a 2-year old try to lie their way out of responsibility for breaking something they know they shouldn't have broken. Children don't *learn* how to lie; they're *born* liars. They just get better at it over time.

I'm also not going to include any Profiles in Tyranny for this section, because it would be unfair. Or more accurately, because I really don't care about being fair, in order to do it right I'd have to do it like this:

Profiles in Tyranny: Everybody Who's Ever Lived in the History of Humankind!

And then I'd have to go and write down the names of everyone who ever lived and mention some of the lies they told other people in an attempt to outsource blame or other gain an advantage over somebody about something. I'd have to start with Plaglak the Caveman, who definitely lied on occasion to his cavebuddies Urk and Grob about the size of the fish he almost caught with his bare hands, and then systematically record every living soul and their various dishonesties. And I just don't want to.

However, in the interest of giving you best possible education in tyranny that I can, I have compiled a selective list of some of my favorite recent lies. Perhaps you'll see some of your favorites in this collection, and perhaps you won't. But please understand, this is not intended to be comprehensive. I could have included literally everyone alive in this compendium if I'd wanted to.

Random Sampling of Some Really Excellent Liars

- **John Edwards** Anyone remember him? You're forgiven if you don't, as his political career is deader than the deadest dead thing that ever died. And why is that? Because of a couple massive lies – specifically, the lie he told to his wife about not having an affair, and the lie he told to the rest of us about not fathering an illegitimate child with the woman he had the affair with. Anybody know what John Edwards is doing these days? Neither do I.

- **Jeffrey Skilling** The former CEO of Enron claimed to have 'no knowledge' of the impending bankruptcy of his own company. Good one, Jeffrey!

- **Bernard Ebbers** The former CEO of WorldCom (noticing a pattern?) was convicted of overseeing approximately $11 billion of accounting fraud. Note to reader: the IRS really, *really* doesn't like it when they find out you've lied to them. And those people have no sense of humor. Seriously. Can't take a joke at *all*.[2]

- **George W. Bush** A month after declaring victory in Iraq nine years too early, the former President of the United States claimed that we had actually found weapons of mass destruction in some of Saddam Hussein's bunkers, a lie repeated so often that even to this day, 20% of Americans believe that we really did find them. Talk about the power of repetition!

An Important Caveat

If you're an astute reader, you might have noticed something about the list of liars mentioned above. All of them - every one of them - eventually got caught. In fact, the history of American business is replete with examples of people getting caught up in the web of their own fabrications. It's not really a matter of *if* you'll get caught, but *when*.

Which leads us to an important point:

Lying doesn't work

It really doesn't, and far less so now than before the age of computers and instant everything. In a world of constant connections, when almost everything is recorded and absolutely every recorded thing can be sent around the world

---

[2] Ebbers also rather famously said "I have nothing to hide" right before pleading the 5th at his first Congressional hearing. If you listen real closely, you can almost hear the sound of Ebbers hiding something.

in a matter of seconds, it is flatly absurd to believe that any lie you tell will stand a reasonable chance of remaining hidden for very long. Sure, it's possible that your lies won't get discovered until after you've retired or died. It's also possible that they will get discovered but will somehow magically not affect you or your career. But odds are your lies will end up hurting you in the long run.

Which begs the question – if lying is a losing long-term gamble, why do it?

The easy answer, of course, is *because you're a tyrant!* But that's a bit too easy for this question. A better answer is that you should lie when you feel like you have no other choice. Lying is the last-ditch effort of a flailing tyrant, a frantic attempt to prevent momentum from swinging against you. Only problem is, in most cases the momentum has already shifted. A well-phrased lie might halt that momentum or slow its progress, but it won't do anything to actually turn things around. Lying doesn't save anything. It only postpones the inevitable day of reckoning.

Oh, and one other thing. Lying will also ensure that nobody ever fully trusts you again – another extremely helpful quality for a tyrant to have.

I realize that this chapter is ending on a bit of a down note, but unfortunately that was inevitable. As I've said a couple times already in this book, most tyrannies eventually fail. By the time you incorporate a healthy dose of lies into your business model, your tyranny will already be on the long downward slide into chaos.

But don't fear. You might be on your way out, but we still need to make sure that you walk away from your tyranny with everything you've worked so hard to acquire. There's still a lot of fun times ahead. Exclamation points galore!!!

Resist Change!!!

Avoid Risk!!!

"If you wait to do everything until you're sure it's right, you'll probably never do much of anything."
Win Borden

Interesting quote, huh? It's even more interesting if you know who Win Borden is – he's a former Minnesota state senator who was convicted in 2004 of tax evasion and sentenced to two years in prison. Apparently he was just waiting to get his tax forms right.

But enough about him. This book is about you, isn't it? And right now you deserve some praise. You now know how to successfully avoid any sense of responsibility for anything that might go wrong in your cold and loveless empire. You've taken credit for others' success, blamed others for your failures, and lied your way through everything else. Couple that with your condescending and insufferable attitude toward your employees, and you have the makings of a mighty fine tyrant.

And yet, the seeds of your destruction have probably already been sown. Even as I write this, Hosni Mubarak is being deposed in Egypt, brought down by a lightning-fast 18-

day revolution that caught everyone by surprise. His power seemed secure - unassailable, even - and yet in under three weeks he has gone from feared dictator to despised outcast. The same thing happened in Tunisia just a few weeks ago, and the same thing will happen in other places around the world again and again and again. At this very moment, Moammar Ghadafi is losing his tyrannical grip on Libya.

Don't let it happen to you.

And thus, the focus of the final section of *Unleash Your Inner Tyrant*! is how to effectively resist change. As far as the tyrant is concerned, change is evil. It is a hideous monster, a slathering wart-faced enemy[1], and you need to fight against it with everything you have. Change is the thing that turns beautiful summer days into frigid winter nights, adorable babies into thieving teenagers, idyllic backyard campfires into out-of-control infernos, healthy tissues into cancerous tumors - I could go on, but I think you see where this is heading.

At its core, change means revolution, and revolution means the potential overthrow of the carefully constructed system that allows the tyrant to remain in power. Conditions changed in Egypt, and Mubarak was removed from power. Things changed in the American marketplace, and hundreds of banks suddenly disintegrated. So if you've done a good job of establishing your tyranny and want it to grow and thrive, nothing should ever change.

So How do You *Do* That?

It's a good question, isn't it? After all, how are you supposed to resist change when things are changing all the

[1] That was a fun phrase for me to write.

time? How can you resist change when everyone around you, those morons that you're forced to work with, keep agitating for it?

Fortunately, I have the answers.

The first thing, of course, is to avoid risk. Risk is the single greatest threat to the reign of a tyrant. Risk means uncertainty, and uncertainty carries with it the potential for failure. To a certain extent, risk and change are synonymous, since you cannot change anything without risking something.

Now I'm sure you're familiar with risk. You have to be, unless you're exactly the same now as you were when you were a baby. Undoubtedly you took risks to get to the position that you're currently in. If you're married, you took a risk by telling your husband or wife that you loved them and wanted to marry them. If you're a mother or father, you took a risk by having children and hoping that things turned out OK. If you've had any professional success of any kind – or even if you've ever managed to get hired – you took a risk by attending your interview and hoping that you wouldn't be laughed out of the office. You've taken all those risks because you had no choice. The only way to move forward in *anything* is to take risks.

But you're not trying to move forward anymore, are you? Of course not! You're right where you want to be, at the top of your tyrannical pyramid. You can see the serfs below your lofty perch, farming the land and fixing their wagon wheels and whatever else it is that serfs like to do. Things are good, and you'd like them to stay that way forever.

Which is exactly why you shouldn't take any more risks. Your goal is to keep things as static and immobile as possible. Will it work? Of course it won't! It's impossible to stop the forward motion of things. But it should prolong your tyranny past its natural lifespan – and it'll definitely make things a lot more fun for you around the office!

Unfortunately, I don't have any *Profiles in Tyranny!* to help guide you through this section. Because as it turns out, it's difficult to find examples of people avoiding something. You can find plenty of pictures online of people who have gotten into car accidents – just Google Image 'car accidents' and several hundred thousand options will present themselves[2] – but it's much harder to find pictures of people who narrowly missed driving themselves through a guard rail. My point is that the art of avoiding risk is essentially a non-action, and it's difficult to find an example of somebody not doing something.

However, I don't want you to worry. Because not acting is just about the easiest thing in the world to do. There are literally hundreds of ways you can avoid risk by doing nothing at all. In fact, by reading this book, some of you are avoiding risk at this very moment!

Interested in other ways to avoid risk? Here you go!

Ways to Avoid All Those Pesky Problems That Just Won't Go Away!!!

- **Surf the Internet** Have you seen all the latest YouTube videos? I'll bet there are a few hundred that you're missing. In fact, there's actually a

[2] Alternatively, you can Google 'redneck car building' and find almost as many examples. Apparently when rednecks see a building, they are compelled to drive their car into it.

website called www.wasteoftime.com. Don't believe me? Check it out for yourself!

- **Do crosswords or play Sudoku** Those little books do a great job of fitting nicely into bigger books. So you can 'attend' meetings without taking a single useful thing away from them. Other than the personal satisfaction that comes from beating the New York Times Sunday puzzle, that is.

- **Take unnaturally long bathroom breaks** This approach has the advantage of being impossible to argue against. If, for example, some audacious soul were to say to you, "You know, you spent an awful long time in the bathroom just now," all you'd have to do is look them straight in the eye and say, "I know I did. And trust me, it wasn't fun for me." End. Of. Discussion.

- **Hide out in your office** A favorite of risk-averse managers everywhere. Because problems can't rear their ugly heads if they can't find you, right? If you need a bit of practice at this one, try to remember back to the time in your childhood when you would cover your eyes during hide-and-seek because you truly believed that if you couldn't see them, they couldn't see you. Same principle.

That should get you started. But all of these approaches, while effective, are also very passive approaches to avoiding risk. The tyrant who adopts these techniques is a bit like a jellyfish, riding the currents wherever they take you. If you want to be active, to make your subordinates fully appreciate your aversion to change, you're unfortunately going to have to talk to them.

Now I know I've already told you to avoid talking to your subordinates as much as possible, but this is one of the only three exceptions to that rule. It's OK to talk to your employees when you want to remind them how far beneath you they are; it's OK to talk to them if you're preparing to criticize them; and it's OK to talk to them when you want to impress upon them how rigid and inflexible you are.

And here's what you should say. Any one of the following is sufficient all by itself, but the best of you will use each of them at least once a week, with an eye toward squeezing them all in once a day.

Sentences of the Terrified!

- **"I don't think that will work."** Notice I don't want you to say *why* you don't think it will work. In fact, it would be best if you don't even let the other person finish talking before you hit them with this zinger. Simple, out-of-hand rejection is what we're shooting for here.

- **"That's not how we do things around here."** Absolutely! Coming up with solutions to problems or inefficient methods is *not how a good company should operate!* Besides, things have always been the exact same at your company forever, haven't they? Since the days of its founding by a single individual or small collection of partners - perhaps in a rented garage, perhaps in a toolshed, perhaps in somebody's basement or living room - nothing at all has changed in any way. So why start now?

- **"That's not part of our culture."** Anybody noticing a theme here?

- **"Don't rock the boat."** This one's a little more aggressive, which of course is why I like it. And never mind that boats are designed for rocking. Never mind that rocking is one of the most soothing motions known to our species. The point is, *SHUT YOUR MOUTH!!!!*

And last, my personal favorite:

- **"Think like that again and I'm calling security."**

Your goal here is to reject ideas, as many ideas as you possibly can. This has the added benefit of reinforcing the notion that you don't care at all what your employees think.

And yet there is one additional piece of mental acrobatics you need to wrap your head around if you want to avoid risk and resist change as effectively as possible. All the best tyrants have mastered this technique, and it is the subject of the next chapter.

So what are you waiting for? Turn the page already. But wait to do it until after you've called security on somebody. Especially those of your coworkers who occasionally wear a thoughtful expression on their faces. Independent thought on the part of your subordinates never leads to anything good, and nothing can wipe the ideas right out of a person's head quite like a well-placed taser jolt.

Trust me. I've been to Mardi Gras – I know what I'm talking about.

Think Short Term!

"We have to choose between a global market
driven only by calculations of short-term profit,
and one which has a human face."
Kofi Annan

"We can do things the cheap way, the simple way, for
the short-term and without regard for the future. Or, we
can make the extra effort, do the hard work, and make
decisions that will cause a better future."
Mike Rounds

"What we're going to do is redouble our efforts
on financial regulatory reform…compensation
should be focused on the long term, so that
you don't have rewards for short-term risk-taking."
Christina Romer

You should have seen this coming – if you thought far enough ahead, that is. But with any good luck, you didn't. If so, you're well on your way to mastering this section without having even read it yet!

As I'm sure you know, one of the best ways to resist change is to not even admit the possibility that change could happen. That's why short-term thinking is so terribly important to the successful career of a tyrant. Because in a short-term view of the world, nothing really changes. Sure, there might be some subtle shifts in one direction or another, but short-term fluctuations never really seem to presage the much larger, world-altering changes that they occasionally lead to.

According to Gary Hamel and C.K. Prahalad, managers spent less than 3% of their time looking to the future

Music to my eyes! With any good luck, you are also spending 3% (or less!) of your time thinking about the things that might be coming down the pipe. You're wearing exactly the right kind of blinders, and I salute you.

Research by Henry Mintzberg found that managers were slaves to the moment, moving from task to task – the median time spent on any one issue was 9 minutes

Seriously, could it get any better? It's awfully difficult to plan for long-term contingencies when you spend more time taking your morning shower than thinking about any particular business issue.

So, what's the secret to short-term thinking? It's pretty simple, and some of the tyrants I've highlighted in previous chapters were excellent examples of this, even if I didn't take the time to point it out to you.

Think Like a Shareholder!!!!!

That's right, my aspiring tyrant. Most shareholders don't care about anything but those next quarterlies, which makes them the perfect role models for this section. Are their company's policies sound and healthy? Who cares! As long as they work *now*. Because as every good shareholder knows, you can always bail out if things start getting ugly.

Some People Are Really, Really Dumb

Now a lot of people don't appreciate the value of thinking like a shareholder. I know it's hard to believe, but it's true. Some businesspeople are simply too stupid to understand the power of the approach I am sharing with you now. The fact that these people have the nerve to call themselves *businesspeople* is an insult to my dignity, and if I could I would challenge them to a duel and prove the supremacy of my thinking by poking them full of sword holes.

Profiles in Idiocy: Jack Welch

Perhaps you've heard of this imbecile, the former CEO of General Electric.[1] He did a lot of things I admire – laying off over 170,000 employees for example, which is the equivalent of firing the entire state of South Dakota – but when it comes to thinking like a shareholder, Welch was a pathetic failure.

But don't take my word for it. This man convicted himself. Listen to what he said in an interview with *Financial Times*:

[1] Emphasis on *former*. What's the problem, Jack, couldn't cut it? Was running a big giant company too hard for you? That's what I thought. Stand aside and let the real leaders through.

"On the face of it, shareholder value is the dumbest idea in the world. Shareholder value is a result, not a strategy."

I think we can all agree that the world is a safer place now that this maniac is no longer in control of anything. There's no telling what kind of damage he might have done to my pocketbook if he'd been allowed to continue.

Profiles in Idiocy: Ken Iverson

It's bad enough that Jack Welch called 'shareholder value' a bad strategy. But Ken Iverson, former CEO of Nucor Corporation[2], had the audacity to compare shareholders to *drug addicts*, of all things. He's delusional! As though anybody could possibly get addicted to money.

What I'm about to print is going to be difficult to read. Steel yourself.

"Many of you, with your short-term view of corporations, remind me of a guy on drugs. You want that quick fix, that high you get from a big spike in earnings. So you push us to take on more debt, capitalize start-up costs and interest,

---

[2] Noticing a trend here? *Former* CEO of GE, *former* CEO of Nucor. Hmm. Looks like listening to these two dopes is a great way to find yourself out of a job.

and slow down depreciation and write-offs. All you're thinking about is the short term. You don't want to think about the pain of withdrawal that our company will face later on if we do what you want."

It's OK. Shhh, shhhh.....I know. Don't cry. It's OK. The bad man is gone now. He's not in charge anymore. I'm here, OK? Don't worry. I'll take care of you. Shhhh......

Now, some misguided dilettantes might be tempted to point out that Iverson helped lead Nucor from near-bankruptcy into one of the most successful steel companies in the country. They might also mention that Jack Welch is one of the most highly respected leaders in American business. And they might use those two pieces of information to suggest – nay, to *insist* – that short-term thinking is a bad approach to running a successful business.

They're right, of course. But that doesn't mean you should listen to them. Why? Because you're not trying to learn how to be a leader. You're reading this book to learn how to be a tyrant. There's a difference.

And that difference is best illustrated in the stories of three people. Or, more accurately, two people and one business.

Profiles in Tyranny: Al Dunlap

You know you're doing something right when your nickname is "Chainsaw Al." You know you've achieved a robust kind of tyranny when several of your vice presidents resign on the day you're appointed CEO. And you know that your place in the pantheon of American business is secure when literally *every* company you oversee loses value over the course of your tenure.

Dunlap probably began his career by extorting lunch money from his fellow classmates, a skill he had perfected by the time he became a businessman. He also must have had a money-laundering business in high school, since he engaged in massive accounting fraud at every company he oversaw. But Al Dunlap is such an accomplished tyrant that we just don't have time to focus on his every action.

So let's get to it – short-term genius. As CEO of Scott Paper Dunlap was so focused on the short-term that he did everything he could to boost current revenues by compromising Scott Paper's ability to function in the long term: he ordered the closure of essential factories, postponed critical maintenance at the remaining factories, and paid attention to nothing but his monthly stock report.

Scott Paper managed to pawn him off on Sunbeam, where Dunlap refined his short-term model. He shuttered 12 of Sunbeam's 18 manufacturing plants and engaged in a favorite practice of his known as 'stuffing the channel,' which encourages buyers to buy more products than they need by offering those products at exorbitant discounts. It's a great short-term strategy – but more importantly, it's terrible in the long term! And, as one might have predicted, in 1998, Sunbeam filed for Chapter 11 protection. As an interesting sidenote, the accounting firm that allowed all of this to happen...Arthur Andersen, which was forced to pay $110 million dollars to settle various shareholder claims.[3]

Dunlap was eventually banned from ever holding an executive position again – just like his protégé, Angelo Mozilo. The two are said to be fast friends and are often seen together, usually in parking garages or all-night pizza joints that never seem to have any business and yet never seem to go under. I tried to learn more, but I was discouraged from doing so by a handful of very large men who persuaded me, on pain of death, not to stick my nose where it doesn't belong.

Profile in Tyranny: Blockbuster Video

Somewhere in your neighborhood, there is a soon-to-be-abandoned building known as Blockbuster Video. You used to visit it often, didn't you? You probably still have a Blockbuster card in your purse or wallet, wedged in between your unused library card and that buy-ten-haircuts-get-one-free card that you never remember to pull out until you're already leaving the hair salon.

There are a lot of uses for an old Blockbuster card. If yours is laminated, it can be an invaluable tool to open a locked door or scrape a thin layer of ice from your windshield. If it is not laminated, it has the power to deliver an annoyingly painful paper cut to an enemy.

[3] Seriously, how on *Earth* does anybody still willingly do business with Accenture?

But one thing it is *not* useful for is renting movies. That's because Blockbuster, in a flash of short-term brilliance, decided that the Internet was probably not going to stay around for very long. They saw Netflix offer unlimited movie rentals that streamed directly to your home, thus saving the time and hassle of driving to a physical location and selecting a single movie. They saw RedBox install kiosks in airports and malls and grocery stores across the country, thus saving the time and hassle of making an additional trip to an additional store in order to rent a movie. They saw this, and Blockbuster said, "This too shall pass."

No one really knows what became of Blockbuster. Some say they took the Twilight Road and left Middle-Earth forever. Some say they wasted away until nothing but their voice remained, echoing forever in caves. Some say they sank into the sea, a promising civilization brought to ruin by the wrath of an angry god.

But whatever happened, they left a record of their passage. And that record is sitting in your wallet right now.

You should really clean out your wallet.

Profiles in Tyranny: Richard McGinn

Those are both excellent examples of the power of short-term thinking. But there's something extra special in the story of Richard McGinn's, former CEO of Lucent[4]. Lucent was spun off of AT&T in 1996, and McGinn was appointed CEO in

[4] Uh-oh. Did I say *former*? I did, didn't I. Well, forget I said that.

1997. The company immediately began growth at a double-digit rate, as did many tech companies in the late 90s. In fact, it was impossible *not* to make money in the late '90s. I was in high school then, and unfortunately I was possessed of the technological acumen of a wilting flower. But if I'd had half a brain, I would have made a single-page website called www.pleasegivemeamilliondollars.com or something equally ridiculous, presented it to investors, and boom! I'd be rich today.

As long as I sold out before 2000, when the whole rising tide became a crushing tidal wave. The dot-com boom-to-bust affected everyone, but especially tech companies. As might have been expected, Lucent's growth began to contract. Hmmm...what to do, what to do?

I know! Let's demand an *increase* in sales by any means necessary. That's what McGinn did, because the shareholders demanded it. His sales team obliged as best they could. But their best wasn't very good, since they were only able to increase sales by offering steep deals and discounts.[5] Thanks for the advice, Mr. Dunlap! As one book I read put it, Lucent was "stealing from the future to meet present shareholder demand." Which is exactly why I burned that book at my first opportunity.

Anyway, McGinn's demands *worked* – in 2000 Lucent actually exceeded its sales targets. However, their short-term success masked a much larger long-term failure. McGinn's policy of counting future sales on current balance sheets

[5] Sound familiar, anyone? Anyone? Bueller, Bueller....

meant that while Lucent met its targets for 2000, they were going to miss their 2001 targets by 20%. Now we're talking!

The end result? McGinn was fired – with a healthy severance package, no doubt – and Lucent was forced to go through a grueling series of cost-saving measures which included the laying off of approximately 39,000 employees.

I know, I know. It's not as impressive a record as Jack Welch laying off 170,000 GE employees. But then again, Lucent was never as large a company as GE. McGinn did the best with what he had, and we shouldn't disparage him just because he wasn't in a position to do more.

Deny Reality by Making Unreasonable Demands!

The story of Richard McGinn leads rather nicely into this concept - denying reality by making unreasonable demands. McGinn's suicidal sales push was borne out of a belief that he could force Lucent to succeed against the entire machine of the American marketplace. He was so dedicated to his short-term philosophy that he allowed for absolutely no backsliding, despite the fact that every company's value rises and falls from time to time.

And you can too.

Tidbits of Happiness for You!

- **Demand increased performance every year – or better yet, every quarter** This will work most effectively for those of you who oversee a sales department. Oh, and feel free to reveal your naked, unrestrained greed when you're exhorting your team to work harder and better. Do you happen to remember that old Warner Brothers' cartoon where Daffy Duck tries to stuff the genie back in the lamp because he wants all the Arabian treasure for himself? If not, look it up on YouTube. Seriously, I don't know why that cartoon is not a standard part of every corporate training program.

- ***Budget* as though performance will increase every year – or better yet, every quarter** To hell with murmurs of recessions, frugality, rising unemployment, and anything else that might hamper your company's growth – your budget should in no way reflect the impending realities of the marketplace. If you are ever having trouble figuring out how to wrap your head around such a short-sighted and ultimately fatal policy, just pay attention every year when the White House releases its annual budget. The fact that they can do so with a straight face is testament to the possibilities of this idea.

That's it, my aspiring tyrant. Short-term thinking doesn't really help you resist change, but it's an excellent way to pretend that change will never come. And really, when you get down to it, are they both the same thing?

Bonus section time!!!

Sucking Like a Champion!

The Hateful Delegator

Hello, and welcome to another installment of *Sucking Like a Champion!* In this section we will teach you how to irritate everyone you work with by delegating jobs to them without their input or permission.

Delegation, of course, is an essential component to effective leadership. Assigning tasks in an intelligent, thoughtful way is usually the best, and often the *only*, way to accomplish anything significant in a reasonable amount of time. Even self-employed people delegate various tasks to an assortment of contractors or part-time employees. Assignments are parceled out to each group member in much the same way a computer routs different functions through different processors in an effort to maximize efficiency.
In other words, delegation is unavoidable.

So, since you're going to be doing it anyway, let's talk about how to do it really, really badly!

The key to effective delegation is to ensure that everyone on the team knows what everyone else is doing – or knows at the very least that everyone else is doing *something*. As long as people believe they are being given an equal share of a shared burden, delegation tends to run smoothly and without a lot of complaint.

However, anybody who ever went to high school or college should know that many group efforts don't work that way at all. I'm sure you've been in groups before where one or two people did all the work while everyone else did nothing. I'll bet you were the lazy one sometimes, and you knew you could afford to be. Why? Because you knew that the high-performing members of your group would pick up your slack, as they wouldn't want to suffer from your lack of effort.

And the same principle applies in business as well.

To get the most mileage out of this, start with minor delegations – asking a colleague to compose a particular email, for example, something so innocuous that nobody could possibly take issue with it. Then you'll want to slowly ramp it up. It's difficult to give specifics when there's no telling what kind of project you'll be working on, but basically you'll want to source every major component of your project – research, intra-office communication, editing, design, testing, market analysis, etc. – to other members of your team. This can most effectively be accomplished through a blizzard of phone calls and emails, a technique that employees the world over have used to make others think that they're actually working. An example follows:

Feel Free to Steal This Sample Email – It's Priceless!

Hey (name),
I'm totally swamped today, and we need the specs for the (whatever you need the specs for) ASAP. Can you get those for me? Thanks!

Note the 'Thanks!' at the end, which functions to turn your question into an ever-so-subtle demand for compliance; after all, who can say no after you've gone to the trouble of thanking them for agreeing to do it? Oh, and did you notice the lack of explanation as to why you're 'totally swamped' today? Which person on your team is going to be rude enough to insist upon the details of your overwhelming workload? None, that's who.

N-O-N-E! MWAH HA HA HA HA!

This email is a true gem, and a few of these every day will ensure that you won't be responsible for anything. If you have no choice but to use the phone as your tool of delegation, make sure you're certain that the person you're calling won't pick up. As long as you never give anybody a chance to question you directly, you should be fine.

Now I realize some of you might look at this and think, "Boy, delegating responsibility sure sounds like a lot of work!" And that's the beautiful thing about this – it *looks* like a lot of work, but it *isn't*. Sure, you might spend an hour every day composing dictatorial emails and phone messages for everyone on your team, but that's not much compared to the eight or ten hours you're supposed to be working. Plus, once you do this for a while you'll realize that manipulating others through incessant delegation is a joy, not a chore. Eventually, if you do it right, it won't feel like work at all.

The real trick, though, is to make sure that your employees have utterly *no* idea what you do. As I said before, as long as people believe they're doing an equal part of a shared burden, they'll be OK. But if you can arrange it so that your employees feel as though they're doing *everything* while you just sit in your office and twiddle your useless thumbs –

remember *Remain Aloof and Above?* – well, that's when the murmurs of mutiny will begin to surface.

And when they do, when the inevitable confrontation comes between you and your overworked and undervalued employees, it will be time for your most important and insidious weapon – the argument that delegation *is* your job! Haven't they seen all the emails and phone calls you've been sending? You've been running yourself ragged trying to keep everybody on task and keep this project on the right timeline, and now somebody has the audacity to question your commitment? The *nerve* of some people!

Enjoy, my aspiring tyrant. It's an exciting world you're about to enter, and I hope you make the most of it.

Create an Escape Plan for You and Nobody Else!

"The next time I say, 'Let's go someplace like Bolivia,' let's go someplace like Bolivia."
Butch Cassidy

Congratulations! By now your tyranny is on the brink of collapse. You've created a toxic working environment, demolished employee morale, and generally made yourself an unwelcome guest at every party you attend. What's more, you've worked hard to ignore the writing on the wall. The end is quite evidently near.

Or perhaps that's not the case. Perhaps your tyranny is humming along at its repressive best. Whatever discontent you've fostered is still silent and impotent, and your strategy of outsourcing blame and hoarding credit is actually helping you attract the attention of some of your superiors. You might even smell a promotion coming! And yet, in the back of your mind you keep hearing those amazingly prescient words of wisdom you read in a fascinating book once upon a time: *most tyrannies eventually fail.* As good as things seem now, it can't hurt to have a back-up plan.

Here's something that should cheer you up, though – at least, if you're one of the top 5 people at your company:

Statistics show that, in most companies, the top five executives receive 75% of the employee stock options.

And do know why the top five executives take an absurdly high percentage of their company's wealth? *Because they can, that's why!*

But that's a bit too easy of an answer. The real reason they do it is because of the statistics I've listed below. Pay careful attention.

After Reading These, You'll Probably Cry Yourself to Sleep

Almost 50% of CEOs in one study had held their jobs for less than three years

In a survey of companies ranging in size from 660 to 900,000 employees, 2 out of 3 installed a new CEO between 1995 and 2000

Nearly 80% of CEOs in 1990 had been replaced within the decade

In the 1990s, 1 in 4 companies went through 3 or more CEOs

The writing is on the wall: things are not going to last forever. You need to prepare yourself for whatever might be coming. So even if your current position seems unassailable, creating an escape plan is a prudent move.

Now perhaps you're wondering how creating an exit strategy is tyrannical. After all, everybody has a retirement account, right? Isn't that essentially an exit strategy of sorts? In fact, isn't it a fundamental tenet of fiscal responsibility to hope for the best and prepare for the worst?

I want you to re-read the title to this chapter. You need to create an escape plan for you *and nobody else!!!!* Let me make myself clear: if you're not profiting at somebody else's expense, then you are not a tyrant. And if you are not a tryant, then we can not be friends. This relationship is simply not going to work, and I'll need you to give me my CDs back, please.

Example Time!

At the risk of making myself sound less omnipotent than I really am, I'm going to admit something to you: this tiny little section took me a long time to write. I spent hours and hours trying to figure out how to teach you the best ways to create an escape plan for you and nobody else, and I eventually had to concede that I was stuck.

And then, a brilliant idea occurred to me. Why *tell* you what to do when I could simply *show* you instead?

Profiles in Tyranny: Richard Fuld

Nicknamed "The Gorilla" both for his competitive business demeanor and the protruding brow ridge on his simian-like forehead, Richard Fuld took the helm of Lehman Brothers when it was spun off of American Express in 1994. For

fourteen years he did a really, really good job, turning a 1993 loss of $104 million into a 2007 profit of $4.2 billion.

Then the whole thing collapsed like a flaming lead balloon. Can lead balloons actually catch on fire? I don't know, but Lehman Brothers sure did!

2007 – $4.2 billion profit

2008 – bankrupt

I'm pretty sure I couldn't burn through $4.2 billion if you gave me eight lifetimes to try it, but Fuld managed to do it in less than a year. Unbelievable. How is he not in politics?

Considering that Fuld had sworn at late as 2007 that Lehman Brothers would not be sold as long as he was alive, one might be tempted to believe that he would do everything he could to save the company he'd helped build up. But Fuld did not go down with his ship. Of course he didn't – what kind of stupid captain does something like that? No, he watched Lehman Brother get sold at auction like an estate sale, then bathed himself in his millions while thousands of his employees lost their jobs. Then he got a job at a hedge fund, then some other banking and investment firm.

Oh yeah – he also transferred his $13.65 million Florida mansion into his wife's name in order to prevent it from being taken in the legal actions that were sure to come. How's *that* for a smack in the face! "That's right, my former employees – good luck finding yourself a cheap apartment to hunker down in. Maybe if you're nice I'll let you stay in a spare room in my mansion. We've been trying to find a decent groundskeeper for a while now, and you might just be the answer to our gardening prayers."

Profiles in Tyranny: Stan O'Neal

Remember Merrill Lynch? Yeah, me either – they got swallowed up in a merger with Bank of America. Guess who drove Merrill Lynch into the ground? But more importantly, guess who got away scot free!

The former CEO of Merrill Lynch, Stan O'Neal is widely credited with holding Richard Fuld's hand as the two men skipped their way down the path of corporate destruction. By overexposing Merrill Lynch to the subprime market, O'Neal helped his company realize a staggering $8 billion loss in *two months* of 2007. And you thought Richard Fuld was impressive! More importantly for our purposes, though, O'Neal earned a whopping $46 million in the same year. And people argue that teachers should get paid based on performance. What a crazy notion! If Merrill Lynch's pay-for-performance policy is anything to go by, our country's teachers would be more handsomely rewarded if they spent their workday forcing their students to rip pages out of their textbooks and recite an erroneous version of the alphabet.

Anyway, O'Neal's abysmal performance eventually got him kicked out of Merrill Lynch. It also managed to get a lot of *other* people kicked out of Merrill Lynch, people who had nothing to do with the company's horrible business model. But most importantly for us, O'Neal's departure was accompanied by a golden parachute worth over $160 million! What's more, he's now on the board at Alcoa, presumably helping that company achieve its stated goal of becoming the worst aluminum conglomerate in the world by 2013.

There are no shortage of people that hate Stan O'Neal. But does O'Neal care? Of course not! Nor does he have to. Because $160 million will buy you a mountain of soundproofing. Not to mention walls, and armed guards, and all the other trinkets that deposed monarchs often surround themselves with.

Profiles in Tyranny: Martin Sullivan

So, let me ask you a question: what would you do if the government plopped down $85 billion to help your company stave off bankruptcy? If your answer is something like, "Use it to help my company stave off bankruptcy," then go shoot yourself in the face with a nail gun a few times until reason returns to you. However, if your answer is something like, "Well, first I'd award myself and my favorite staff members several million dollars in unwarranted compensation to make up for all the money we lost when we drove our company in the ground," then give yourself a pat on the back.

Martin Sullivan is the *wunderkind* who helped AIG shrink from a $100 billion company in 2006 to a $4 billion outfit in 2009. His catastrophic business acumen ultimately led to his ouster, but not before he'd given himself an iron-clad contract that provided him with millions in severance *as well as millions more after he had already departed the company!* That's right – Sullivan's escape plan was so ingenious that he continued to get paid after he was officially no long on AIG's payroll![1]

[1] To be fair, he probably did less damage off the payroll than on it.

Oh, and one more thing: the guy was *knighted* by the British crown. Seriously. To be fair, his knighthood took place before AIG went from awesome to awful. But still, that's pretty cool. I wouldn't be surprised if Stan O'Neal has already asked about how to hook up a knighthood for himself. And knowing what I know about Martin Sullivan, I think he'll be happy to oblige.

As you might have guessed, there is something of a formula here. To put it simply, the higher up you are in the company, the more successful your escape plan is likely to be.

So, the *first* step to creating an escape plan for you and nobody else is to work your way into a senior position at whatever company you work for. This will take time. Most of the best tyrants slogged away in the trenches for a decade or more before finally getting themselves into the enviable position I am hoping you'll find for yourself. If you want to learn how to move up in your company, you should probably consult another book. Or, you can follow this very simple three-step guide:

Three Steps to a Senior Position!

Step One: Cut down those beneath you.

Step Two: Suck up to those above you.

Step Three: Repeat.

It's not a tough model to follow.

And once you've made that happen for yourself, these are the steps to follow to ensure that you walk away unscathed from the havoc you're about to wreak[2] on your officemates:

Step-by-Step Escape Plan Guide

- **Insist on severance guarantees in your contract** Get yourself a good lawyer, and argue every point. Most people will eventually concede to your demands if you remain intractable for long enough. Besides, why would they need to worry about anything? It's not like you're planning to run your company into the ground and then bail out, right?

- **Perform so horribly that the company buys out your contract to prevent you from doing any more damage** Remember Al Dunlap? Remember Stan O'Neal? Remember Martin Sullivan? Yeah, I thought you might.

- **Do not, under any circumstances, allow your compensation package to be related to your company's performance** As I've already mentioned, pay-for-performance initiatives are for teachers and other minimum-wage earners, not tyrants like you.

- **Insist on lavish bonuses for meeting performance goals** Don't you just love having it both ways? I sure do. Try it sometime – it's fun!

---

[2] I think it's unfair that the only thing it's possible to wreak is havoc. You can't wreak joy, or compassion, or understanding. I want to be a joywreaker, darnit!

- **Leave on a down note** Walking away with giant bags of money is not nearly as much fun if everybody else is doing the same. If everyone had a Ferrari, nobody'd be excited about owning a Ferrari. So time your departure to coincide with massive layoffs, furloughs, bonus cancellations, hiring freezes, mandatory overtime, the elimination of 401K matching, or some other piece of bad news. Otherwise you just won't feel special.

- **Do not allow shareholders to vote on your compensation package** Who do those vagabonds think they are, anyway, trying to tell you how much you should be getting paid? The arrogance - the *nerve* of those people. They act like they own the place!

- **Consider investing in an escape pod** They have them in movies, and it always looks cool when somebody jettisons to safety in one. Plus it gives you a great excuse to use the word 'jettison,' which almost never happens.

There are other techniques, too, but these should get you started on creating an iron-clad escape plan in case everything should go right down the crapper.

Which leads us to our final point. Occasionally the best laid plans of mice and men go awry.[3] And if that should

---

[3] Or, if you prefer that I quote the poem in its original Scottish, occasionally the best laid plans of mice and men 'gang aft agley.' Anybody wonder why Scottish is not an oft-spoken language? I don't.

happen to you…if the changing times should overwhelm your every effort to resist them and start taking you and your company in a direction you have not carefully orchestrated…if you find yourself surrounded by new people, new technologies, new ideas, and new ways of doing things…if the repressive autocracy you've worked so hard to create starts to crash down around your ears…then there's only one thing left for you to do.

When All Else Fails… Company Sabotage!!!!

"An annihilation that only man can provoke,
only man can prevent."
Elie Wiesel

The time has come. By this point in your journey, many of your brethren have already fallen by the wayside. Some have failed to manage their tyranny effectively and have been ousted from power by a popular uprising. Others are safely ensconced on their temporary thrones, enjoying the fruits of power and oblivious to the uprising that looms just over the horizon. Still others have begun their steady fall from grace and are frantically trying to avoid the inevitable through lies, misdirection, creative accounting, and whatever else they can think of. But those will only postpone their eventual day of reckoning. You know that better than most, don't you? Because if you're still reading this book, then you've already been there. You've been to the mountaintop, and now you're sitting at rock bottom.

But you don't have to sit there alone. There is still this one path left you, the one path that only the best of tyrants dares to follow. And you already know what it is.

That's right. If you're going to go down, then you'd better take everyone else with you.

This is going to be a short section, because I cannot tell you how to do what needs to be done. There is no formula to follow, no step-by-step process other than what I've outlined for you in previous chapters. It's quite possible that you've done everything in this book and still will not have an opportunity at company sabotage. As Lenin said, a successful revolution requires revolutionary times, and perhaps your company is simply not at a tipping point. And even if you've followed every facet of my peerless strategy, I can still promise you nothing more than that there is a good possibility your company will be on the verge of collapse.

But if that does indeed happen to be the case, it will be up to you to take that final, irrevocable step. Much like the straw that breaks the camel's back or the soft sound which triggers an avalanche, your final act of tyranny very well throw everyone and everything you know into chaos.

Now let's make one thing clear. I'm not talking about simple destruction here. Milton set Initech on fire in *Office Space*, which might seem like an effective form of sabotage. But buildings can be re-built. New employees can be hired, new customers can be acquired, new equipment can be purchased, and voila! Before you know it, a phoenix rises from the ashes of its deceased predecessor.

No, my aspiring tyrant. When I speak of company sabotage, I mean destruction of a different sort. I'm talking about wholesale slaughter, the kind of action that will forever and always bar your company from ever doing business again. I'm talking about the kind of sabotage from which it is impossible to recover, the kind of thundercloud in which there is no silver lining.

And our role model here?

Profiles in Tyranny: Stuart Parnell

Anybody remember this guy? He came and went pretty quickly, but he left a delightful impression on the business world. Stuart is the former President and CEO of Peanut Corporation of America (PCA), which in 2009 was found to be responsible for a salmonella outbreak that sickened over 700 people, killed at least nine, and led to the largest food recall in U.S. history, affecting over 350 companies and more than 3,900 food products. He made a bit of a name for himself by sending out an email (later leaked to the press) complaining about how much money the salmonella problem was causing PCA, and then made a slightly bigger name for himself by answering every question at his Congressional hearing, no matter how minor, with a recitation of his rights under the Fifth Amendment. It's good to see that you can get at least one thing right, Stu!

Today PCA is...well, it's not really an *is* anymore. It's a was, a has-been, a phantom. Gone, broke, nada, nowhere. Their buildings are probably housing a small but thriving population of indigent boxcar people. PCA's 2011 earnings outlook is considered by many to be 'slightly worse than that dude selling imitation watches on the corner.' I think you get the point.

But Parnell's tyranny goes far beyond the destruction of his own company. Because after the salmonella outbreak, consumers reacted as they usually do during a food scare – by avoiding peanuts altogether, a reaction which is estimated to have cost the peanut industry over $1 billion in lost revenue (PCA's annual revenue in 2008, by way of comparison, was $25 million.) The public's perfectly understandable overreaction thus affected the livelihoods of untold numbers of peanut growers, producers, and distributors who had absolutely nothing to do with PCA or its life-threatening products. Which means Stuart Parnell managed to destroy the livelihoods of people with whom he had absolutely no business relationship – how's *that* for thorough!

So, what was Stuart's secret? Perhaps it was that he so focused on short-term gains that he willfully ignored the pressing need to repair his processing facilities. Perhaps it's that he authorized the shipment of products that had previously tested positive for salmonella. Perhaps it's that he then denied any knowledge of positive salmonella tests among their products despite the fact that at least 12 such tests in 2007 and 2008 confirmed its existence. Perhaps it's that factory conditions were so deplorable that PCA employees are quoted as having said they would not allow their own children to eat PCA products. Perhaps it's that one of PCA's processing plants in Texas was never even authorized as a food manufacturing facility. Perhaps it was something else entirely that I'm not even aware of. Or perhaps it was all of these things and more.

There are several lessons to be gathered from all this, but I think the most important of them is this: if you happen to live in Stuart Parnell's neighborhood whenever he puts his place up for sale, you'd better hope he finds a buyer. Because he's the kind of man who just might start a wildfire and destroy every home in his neighborhood just so he could collect on his homeowner's policy. I'm not saying he will, but I certainly don't think it's beyond him.

And I don't even want to *think* about what he'd do if he and his wife ever had trouble getting pregnant.

Lock your doors, people. Lock your doors.

Gentle reader, Stuart Parnell is a man after my own heart. This is man who put profit before conscience, a man who refused to see the writing on the wall until that wall came crashing down around him. He deserves our careful study and praise. He deserves a statue somewhere, if for no other reason than because it would be fun to watch his former employees tear it down.

But it seems unfair to give him all the glory. After all, there are so many whose stories we could have chosen. And I'd hate to leave anybody out who deserves your adulation. So here it is for you, my aspiring tyrant, presented for your edification…

The Symphony of Awesomeness!!!

- **Ken Lay!** Congratulations, buddy! He ran a company that once posted $26 billion in earnings *in a single quarter!* This is a company that sold something literally everyone wants, a company that had far more demand than supply. And yet, he managed to destroy the whole thing. I can only assume that it was one of Ken Lay's ancestors who gave the *Titanic* its final inspection before it went off on its maiden voyage.

- **Richard Fuld!**[1] Uh-oh! Looks like somebody put all his money on one number at the roulette table! I'd be willing to bet that both Lehman brothers would be turning in their graves – if their gravesites hadn't been auctioned off to cover Richard Fuld's mistakes, that is!

- **Angelo Mozilo!** I'm just going to put this out there, Angelo – I think Countrywide's investors would have appreciated you a lot more if you'd spent a little less time on your tan and a little more time paying attention to the market. But then again, you *did* pay attention to the market, didn't you? You just chose to create a market that was fundamentally unsustainable. Oh well, no big deal – I mean it's not like anybody lost their house over it or…wait a second...oh.

I know I'm missing several tyrants whose names deserve a place of honor on this list, and I apologize for any and all omissions – they are unintentional and solely the result of my ignorance, and I'm certain that in future editions of *Unleash Your Inner Tyrant!* the Symphony of Awesomeness will swell to truly awesome proportions.

---

[1] I know I've already mentioned him – twice, actually – but I'm mentioning him again. After everything he's done, the guy deserves a couple encores.

And yet, these few are enough. These visionaries had the courage to sink their own ship rather than let the enemy take control. They knew the truth that I am trying to impart to you – that success is not a team effort, *but failure is!!!* They knew that if you're going to go down, you might as well make the rest of the world hate you while it happens. And they knew that, when you really get down to it, a grand jury trial really isn't all that bad – especially if you die before they get to the verdict!

But here's the most important lesson, my aspiring tyrant. If you've paid attention to everything I'd taught you up to this point, then maybe someday you too can address the press corps on the steps of a courthouse while angry protestors are held back by a wall of riot police. Maybe you, too, can commission a limousine to drive you to your Congressional hearing while the people whose lives you destroyed ride the city bus to the unemployment office. *That*, people, is what I call a good Thursday.

So there it is! You now know how to create the proper environment of fear, self-interest, and mistrust. You know how to trample your underlings and crush any desire they might once have had to excel at work and go above and beyond. You know how to take credit for other people's successes, blame others for your failures, and lie your way out of any intractable problems that crop up. And you know how to resist the hydra-headed demon baby of inexorable change. Thus it is with great honor that I am able to pronounce each of you who have actually read this entire book…

Unfit to Lead!!!!!

Morally Reprehensible!!!!!

Hope You Never Have Children!!!!!

Pretty Certain Prison Clothes Will Suit Your Complexion!!!!!

Congratulations! Give yourselves a hand! Pat yourself on the back - or better yet, find a subordinate to pat you on the back for you! You are now free to make everybody who works with and for you loathe the fact that they do! Huzzah I say! Huzzah again! And again, HUZZAH!!!!!

What You Really Need to Know

The Truth About Leadership

"Take my building equipment,
all my money, my land,
but leave me my people,
and in one year I will be on top again."
Andrew Carnegie

It should be obvious that my advice up to this point has been terrible. It sucks, don't take it, do the opposite, that's the real message. And now my secret is revealed![1]

I'm going to go out on a limb here and assume that you don't actually want to be a tyrant. I'm guessing you don't want your employees to loathe the sight of you, to talk about you behind your back, to write tell-all memoirs or blog posts once they quit or retire about the suffering they had to endure under your nightmarish regime. I'm guessing you, like most other people, want to do right.

And yet, there is certainly no shortage of bad leaders. In the last several years I've spoken to hundreds of groups,

---

[1] Did I really have to say that? Unfortunately, yes I did.

from mom-and-pop outfits up to Fortune 50 giants; and when I sent out a request to some of my contacts in those companies asking for stories about bad bosses to include in this book, I got a *lot* of responses. Eager ones, sent to me by people who were thrilled to have an opportunity to vent about some of the headaches they've had to endure. I haven't included all of them in this book, and I've changed everyone's name so that nobody would get in trouble for being honest – but take my word for it, finding real-life stories to share with you was hands-down the easiest part of writing this book.

One story in particular stands out, though. Not because it's unique, because it isn't; it's actually the most common kind of story that I received from people. But it stands out as a thorough, start-to-finish example of the consequences, both personally and professionally, of bad leadership. I've done almost no editing to this story, except to pull out details that might identify who sent this to me.

Storytime!

Dear Jeff,

I am grateful to HAVE a job, however unsatisfying it is in virtually every way. In the beginning, my boss presented himself as spiritual, diligent, caring, and dedicated. Over the years, I've come to see through the fog of his personal fraud (not criminal), and I find it hard to respect what he does.

So here is my horror story. I am part time, less than 32 hours a week, and usually in the 20s. Hours have gone down over the past 3 years. He's kind of a dilettante and if he paid more attention to his work and had me on task with things that actually apply to my job description, I'd be better employed (as in a real workweek) and happier. He works at home, and calls me to patch him through on phone calls to clients so that they think he is in the office. Rather than quick emails for task requests, he leaves me 57,000 endlessly rambling and repetitive phone messages, despite my explaining how unworkable this is for things that need to actually be in writing. My husband overheard me checking my messages one day and asked: "Is that really what he does every day?" And I had to reply, "Unfortunately, yes."

The ridiculousness reaches its peak at Christmastime. I have worked for this person for 4 years. I don't make enough money to support myself – remember, I'm part-time, and hours have gone down every year – but he EXPECTS a both a Christmas and a birthday gift, because they occur within days of each other. And I catch a rash of %^&* if it doesn't happen. The past two Christmases in a row he has complained about what I got him. It is INFANTILE. For my Christmas compensation, I get NO paid time off for any reason, at any time. My Christmas compensation has actually DECREASED since I began, rather than increased, even though market conditions have turned around. I am way underemployed, but it is difficult to find something else right now. I keep trying though.

And if I left, he wouldn't know where anything is in the information system. He has no clue about any of the government compliance matters that I manage, or how it is maintained. And I do the taxes too. He'd be up @#$% Creek. He could never train my replacement because he chooses to stay clueless about my contribution to his being able to live a life of leisure.

Want more? How about this. When I was in a wheelchair for months with a broken ankle, unable to drive and cabbing it everywhere, he expected me to oversee the moving of our entire office, by myself, to a new location while renovations were being done at our old office, and then back in again. He even complained when I didn't make it back and forth fast enough. I had to get on medication to cope with his incessant stupidity during this time, one of the most trying times in my life. Otherwise I'd have told him off and gotten fired. It was during this time, when I was most strapped for money with NO BENEFITS, and not enough to make it on, that he threw his first tantrum about not getting a Christmas gift. With the medical bills/out-of-pocket expenses I was dealing with, my FAMILY was not even getting gifts from me that year.

I have come to be THE I.T. person in house, or things that need fixing on the computers doesn't get done. That's part of the problem, I guess; I've shown an ability to get things done, so he expects me to learn how to do many technical things that are not really part of my job as a secretary, just because I'm intelligent and able – and all of them with no more compensation or consideration for the value I add.

The guy is insular and clueless. What he doesn't realize is how screwed he would be if I left with no notice.

This, in a nutshell, sums up the consequences of tyranny. You have an intelligent, capable woman who *wants* to work, and her boss is systematically destroying that desire in her. She stays at her job because she feels like she has to –

but that won't always be the case. She'll keep looking, and eventually something better, or maybe just something *else*, will come along. And when it does, she's not going to hesitate. She's not going to weigh options. She's going to jump at the chance, and her boss is going to be left completely unprepared.

But perhaps you think she's misrepresenting herself. After all, frustrated employees always talk about how essential they are and how bad things would be if they were to leave. To listen to them tell it, every employee is the only thing keeping your company from imploding. Surely they're overstating their importance, right?

Perhaps not. Consider this - it's a statistic you might be familiar with (mostly because I used it earlier in the *Talk More Than You Listen!* chapter), but even so, I think it's significant enough that it bears repeating:

In a study of 500 mangers in North America, 75% of them reported knowing employees within their company whose unique knowledge would be lost if they left the company

Make no mistake. Unless you work in an industry where literally *anyone* could do the jobs that need doing, your coworkers and employees are essential to your success. In most cases, the better you treat them, the better you'll be rewarded. If you treat them poorly though, chances are it will eventually come back to haunt you.

And if you somehow still don't believe me, do yourself a favor and talk to a self-employed person sometime. You might think that the very fact of their self-employment would suggest that they don't need anyone else's help. So ask them and see if that's the case. If even *one* self-employed person tells you that they don't rely upon others to make their business a success, I'll give you a trillion dollars.

A Case for Tyranny?

And yet, that doesn't mean you can't be a quite successful bad boss. I think it's important to point out that being a tyrant in no way prevents you from being a leader. All of the people I've mentioned as tyrants in this book are leaders, and almost all of them were (or are) extremely successful. Some of them had that success taken from them – Al Dunlap, for example, engaged was by all account a tyrannical person both personally and professionally, and he was eventually barred by the SEC from ever holding a corporate office again. John Edwards had his political career destroyed by the lies he was caught telling. Harold Geneen micromanaged ITT into an early grave. Bob Nardelli was forced out at Home Depot.

But at the same time, each of these men are still extremely wealthy. And plenty of people with tyrannical qualities – Ralph Ellison and Rupert Murdoch, for example – have achieved a phenomenal level of success that shows no sign of slowing down. It's possible that their hubris, lack of trust, poor treatment of their employees, or some other undesirable leadership quality will eventually catch up with them; there's no shortage of billionaires who have ended their lives in prison. But it's also possible that they'll remain successful billionaires for the rest of their lives.

The point is, each of these people is a leader. Each of them is successful. But in almost every case, they're not the kind of leaders you and I would want to follow.

The Dilemma

So we're at a bit of an impasse. On the one hand, there's the kind of leader that we all know we're supposed to be - attentive, patient, demanding yet understanding, honest, accountable, you know the list of adjectives. And on the other hand there are very visible examples of people who take an entirely different path and manage to find exceptional rewards. There are authors who've made the argument that people like Ralph Ellison and Rupert Murdoch have achieved their level of unbelievable success specifically *because* of their tyrannical leadership styles. And given the personal fortune of people like Richard Fuld - who even to this day denies having done anything wrong in leading Lehman Brothers straight into catastrophe - the argument that tyranny leads to personal success is certainly one that cannot be ignored.

So what is the best way to proceed? Should you listen to all the advice you've been given in all the leadership lectures you've attended and business books you've read - or should you follow the example of the tyrants in this book and attempt to find your success by following their model?

It's a question I can't answer for you. Only you can decide the path that best suits who you are and what you want. But based on your answer to the following question, I can absolutely tell you which path you'll choose:

Where is your loyalty?

If I had to distill this book down into a single sentence, that would be the one. Where is your loyalty – to yourself, or to your company? The people I've highlighted as tyrants were loyal to themselves first and to everyone else a very distant second. For them, the ends have always justified the means, success has always been its own reward regardless of the costs, and other people have always been a necessary but expendable evil. And if that describes you, then you've already chosen your path. You can stop reading this book now. Chances are you're not going to like anything else that I have to say.

The alternative, however, is to be loyal to your company. And by *company* I do not mean the industry you work in, the building where you do that work, or the products that you sell – those things comprise your *business*, and very very few of us are loyal to a business. If you work in banking, I doubt you said to yourself as a child, "Man, I really love counting other people's money, and I can't wait to share my love of competitive interest rates with others." If you work in agriculture, I doubt you have a deep, intrinsic passion for grain elevators. No child has ever said, "When I grow up, I want to work in a cubicle!" By *company* I'm talking about the other people who make your industry and building and products into a living thing – your customers, your colleagues, your superiors, your subordinates, all of their families.

Who are you loyal to? A tyrant's loyalty is to him or herself. But if there is any part of you that genuinely cares about the other people you work with, then you'll encourage an environment where they feel appreciated and valuable.

And you know what? Chances are you do care about them. I've asked literally thousands of people in probably a hundred different industries whether they like or dislike their jobs. Some enjoy what they do, and others don't. But in *every* case, when I ask them to explain why they do or don't like their job, the answer includes a discussion about the people they work with. In many cases, people who enjoy their bosses and coworkers find themselves happy in a job that wouldn't otherwise interest them. Conversely, people who dislike their bosses and coworkers often dislike jobs that involve work they would otherwise very much enjoy. And when I ask self-employed people about the difficulties they've faced in their chosen career, all of them – 100% of them – mention their lack of coworkers as a downside to going into business for yourself. Almost all of us want to be connected to others. And so I'm guessing that you actually do care about the people you work with, and that you also care how they feel about you.

Job satisfaction surveys always claim that salary and benefits are the most important factors in determining whether or not people enjoy their jobs. But that statistic is slightly misleading. Because when people are asked what salary they would be comfortable with, people routinely name a figure around twice their current income, *regardless what their current income is.* Here's another interesting discovery about money: while there is a correlation between a person's income and his/her happiness, that correlation stops after $75,000. In other words, a person making $250,000 a year, or $1,000,000 a year, or $50,000,000 a year, will not believe their wealth to be contributing any more to their happiness than someone making $75,000 a year. So while it is true that salary and benefits definitely contribute to a person's sense of well-being, its power has an upper limit.

In the end, it is that community of individuals that shapes who we are and how we feel about the world we've attached ourselves to. So if you expect to lead anybody, whether it's one employee or one million, you're going to need to take their thoughts, ideas, feelings, and concerns into consideration.

The Power of Leadership

You're probably familiar with the Milgram experiments, a famous psychological study in which subjects were instructed to press a button that would supposedly shock an unseen person whenever that person answered a question incorrectly. In reality there were no shocks, and the person pretending to be shocked was an actor. Each subject was accompanied by an instructor who continually encouraged them to administer shocks of increasingly higher voltage. The experiment is famous because, despite the fact that each subject believed he was delivering an increasingly painful amount of electricity to another person – and indeed, was allowed to hear their victim screaming and begging them to stop – 65% of participants continued to shock their victims as long as the instructor kept encouraging them to. Milgram's experiment demonstrated that many people will act in a way contrary to their own beliefs as long as they're being told to do so.

However, you might not be familiar with a less well-known version of the Milgram experiment designed to demonstrate how quickly people conform to the actions of others. In this version, each subject was accompanied by two others, both actors, who were also instructed to administer shocks to an unseen victim. In some cases, the actors refused to participate; in others, they did so willingly. The results are significant: those subjects who saw two other people administering shocks agreed to shock their own victims 90% of the time, while subjects who watched two others refused to participate agreed only 10% of the time.

Taken together, the Milgram experiments show the power of leadership. People want to follow a leader - it's a desire that's bred into almost all of us. So if you are in a position of leadership, it's up to you to give your people something worth doing, to provide them with a model that they can be excited to follow. And chances are, you won't really know what that model should look like until you've talked to the people you're leading to see what their thoughts and ideas are.

Leadership *is* Communication

I've read way too many business books. I'm guessing you have, too. Like you, I get them from presenters at conferences, or I buy them after recommendations from friends. Most of them have numbers in the title: the 21 Steps to a Better You, or the 18 Secrets of Rockstar Leadership. I've always been amused by those titles, partially because their formula reminds of a Cosmo cover (37 New Ways to Make Him Wild For You!).[2] But those titles are also slightly disingenuous. Because when you get down to it, there's only one key to successful leadership: communication.

---

[2] Just a tip, Cosmo readers: there aren't any new ways to make men wild for you. We're perfectly happy with the same old ways we've been happy with for the last billion years. We men are simple creatures, which I'm sure is something you've known all along.

If you'll look back over the chapter titles of this book, you'll realize that every one of them deals directly with one of the following two concepts:

How well or poorly do you communicate with others?

How well or poorly do you allow others to communicate with you?

Even chapters like *Dress Like an Autocrat, Remain Aloof and Above,* and others that don't mention communication are in fact addressing that very subject. A lack of communication is still a form of communication; you can tell people all kinds of things simply by withholding information. You can read as many business books as you want, but every one of them is going to tell you the same thing. Communication is *the* key. Leadership, as it turns out, is not a terribly complicated subject.

Do you want to be a well-respected leader, the kind of boss that others are excited to work for and want to impress, the kind of manager whose employees consistently exceed their set goals and expectations? Then you absolutely *must* create an environment in which your employees feel free to speak, to share their thoughts and ideas, to challenge you when they think there might be a better way.

My Favorite Business Example

I know some of you don't want to. Some of you probably do subscribe to Douglas MacGregor's Theory X; some of you probably believe that your employees need to be kept on a short leash in order to prevent them from causing you or your company damage. And if that does describe you, let me share with you my favorite business example of the power of open channels of communication between managers and the employees they manage.

My favorite story is about Jack Welch. Everybody cites Welch as one of the best leaders of the past 50 years. He is always held up as a symbol of how to do it right, and I believe he still gets six figures to go somewhere and deliver a speech about leadership. And while I routinely get seven figures to do the same, I'm still think Welch's fee is impressive.

Anyway, there's something interesting about Welch's career that I've heard almost nobody ever mention. In his first ten years as CEO of General Electric, he was ranked fifth out of seven among GE's CEOs in terms of return on equity. *Fifth* out of *seven* – comfortably in the bottom half. Not terribly impressive for a man that most people consider to be one of the best leaders of the past 50 years.

Welch spent his first eight years at General Electric creating the model that would be become the standard for American business in the 1990s. Vowing that GE would not participate in any business in which it did not hold the #1 or #2 spot, he slashed and burned, selling off hundreds of companies and cutting more than 170,000 jobs. (This, by the way, is the exact same approach to business that other less-beloved leaders like Al Dunlap also practiced.[3]) Fortune Magazine named him the 'toughest boss in America' in 1984,

---

[3] Although Dunlap and several others added an element of massive accounting fraud to their business model which Welch somehow managed to overlook. Yet one more reason that Welch is obviously not as great as everyone else claims him to be.

and eventually his relentless scorched-earth management style earned him the nickname "Neutron Jack," in honor of the neutron bomb, a theoretical weapon that could kill people while leaving buildings intact. I've read one book that credits Welch with inventing the concept of 'downsizing.' But whether he did or not, one thing is clear: if you were a GE employee from 1981 to 1989, you probably didn't have a whole lot of job security. In those first eight years, Welch was the quintessential top-down manager, deciding from his corporate suite what was best for a company whose industries covered everything from washing machines to missiles.

Then, in 1989, while attending a conference, Welch had a conversation with a business professor. The professor acknowledged that Welch had done an excellent job of getting people out of General Electric, then followed up with a question: "So when are you going to get the work out?" This seemingly ambiguous question ultimately led Welch to create the Work-Outs, a program that basically boils down to this:

"What would happen if we ask our employees what they think we should do?"

(Side note: that this was considered a groundbreaking concept in 1989 blows my freaking mind. I have three employees and work occasionally with about a dozen others, and if I didn't ask those people what they thought we should do as we attempt to move forward, I'd be working with nobody really, really quickly. Seems like a pretty obvious approach. But then again, that explains why I get seven figures a speech and Welch only gets six.)

Anyway, Welch soon implemented the Work-Out model across every one of General Electric's companies. In his own words: "The idea was to hold a three-day, informal town meeting with 40 to 100 employees from all ranks of GE. The boss kicked things off by reviewing the business and laying out the agenda, then he or she left. The employees broke into groups, and aided by a facilitator, attacked separate parts of the problem. At the end, the boss returned to hear the proposed solutions. The boss had only three options: the idea could be accepted on the spot, rejected on the spot, or more information could be requested."

And two things happened. First, the Work-Outs proved to be extremely popular. This should come as no surprise, since people everywhere are quite fond of telling others what they think should be done. So on the one hand, the Work-Outs were an excellent way to improve morale and foster a heightened sense of teamwork and shared success.

The second thing that happened is this: GE's net income went from $3.9 billion in 1989 to $5.9 billion in 1994. That is a 51% increase, virtually unheard of in a corporation that size. And in 1994, General Electric was the most profitable of the largest 900 corporations in the United States.

Perhaps you were already aware of this. If you were, then you've probably read the standard line about why General Electric was able to turn such an impressive profit in those five years under Welch's leadership. The standard line is that Welch aggressively divested GE's low performing companies, thus streamlining the organization and leaving it with a collection of high-performing companies that thus allowed GE to achieve that kind of unprecedented growth. That's what most people say, and that very well may be true.

But here's my question: were those low-performing companies underperforming because they were inherently flawed, or because Jack Welch had not yet hit upon the management style that would have made them all profitable?

Here's what I think. If Jack Welch had thought to ask GE employees in 1981 what they thought could be done to improve things, most of those 170,000 layoffs would not have been necessary. I'm not saying he was a bad leader. But I *am* saying that I think he wasted a good portion of eight years trying to do everything himself or through the heads of his various divisions before figuring out that maybe GE's employees – the people on the ground, the ones staring every day at the problems they were dealing with – might have a few good ideas of their own.

Fun Question Time!

So let me ask you a question I asked you earlier in this book:

When was the last time one of your employees directly contradicted you?

Take a second and think back. Did it happen this week? This month? Can you remember at all?

Now, let me ask you another question:

When was the last time your *spouse* directly contradicted you?

I'd ask you to take a second and think back, but I know I don't need to. It happened today, didn't it? Or last night. Perhaps yesterday afternoon, maybe at breakfast. *IT*

HAPPENS EVERY DAY OF YOUR MARRIED LIFE!!!! I know it does. Your spouse never *stops* disagreeing with you. Marriage would be so much easier if your spouse did not have a brain, and independent thoughts – because that brain and those thoughts get in the way of what you want to do.

Your spouse contradicts you all the time – I know they do. Not in a bad way, necessarily, but in a 'I think we should do it like this' kind of way. And do you know why they do that? Because they don't fear you. Your relationship with your spouse is equal, or relatively equal, as it has to be if you're going to have a long and healthy relationship with that person.

And the same rules that govern personal relationships are the ones that need to govern your professional relationships. Now obviously you're going to have a different kind of relationship with your boss, or coworker, or employee, than you do with your husband or wife. But if open communication is the key to a successful marriage, then it is also the key to a successful business relationship.

This May Come as a Surprise

And you know something? Your employees *want* to participate. They *want* to be heard. There isn't a person alive who doesn't want to know that they're being heard and appreciated. There isn't a person alive who doesn't have ideas about how they think things should be done. And there isn't a person alive who doesn't want to feel important in some way.

And if you think that isn't true of your employees, then chances are you've never asked them. Remember, the average total time managers spend discussing each employee's style and performance is approximately four hours per employee per year. But more to the point, fewer than 40% of employers *ever* have a conversation with their employees that addresses any of the following questions:

- **What do you enjoy about your job?**
- **What don't you enjoy about your job?**
- **If you could, how would you improve your working situation?**
- **What do you see as your particular strengths?**
- **What goals do you have for your professional future?**

A good number of these questions get addressed in one way or another at the interview, but then most of the time they're never brought up again. And they need to be. If you want to have engaged employees, you're going to have to engage them.

So take a moment and ask yourself if you're really listening to your employees. Are you giving them an opportunity to do what they do best every day? If you're not, don't feel bad – you're in the majority. But now's the time to change.

And the reward? Consider this: Gallup polled 198,000 employees working in 7,939 business units within 36 companies. The poll asked respondents to answer the following question: *At work, do you have the opportunity to do what you do best every day?* When employees answered 'strongly agree' to this question, they were 50% more likely to work in business units with lower employee turnover, 38% more likely to work in more productive units, and 44% more likely to work in units with higher customer satisfaction scores.

Whether you realize it or not, your employees adjust themselves to mirror your leadership style. If you are close-minded and mistrustful, the working environment your employees create will reflect that. If you are open, attentive, responsive, and adaptable, that attitude will trickle down.

Forging open lines of communications will also allow you to better handle difficult conversations when you're forced to have them. Chances are you have some employees who are less than fully productive. They check out before they even arrive to work, go through the motions, do what's necessary and nothing more - and sometimes you let it go. Perhaps you think it's easier to say nothing.

But what do you have to lose? What do you have to lose by taking that employee aside and saying, "Listen, I know you're not happy here. I know you're not fulfilled. And I want to know why. I want to know what we can do to make you happy. Because unfortunately, I'm not getting what I need from you. So right now neither of us are happy, and that's not OK. So let's talk, let's figure this out." In many cases your dissatisfied employees need little more than an opportunity to have that conversation, to analyze the causes of their unhappiness and search for a better path.

You might also be thinking that such a conversation is asking for a fight. And in all honesty, it might be. Some of your disengaged employees have so fully checked out that the idea of reconciliation will seem almost offensive to them. Some people find an odd comfort in their misery, and they won't be interested in a solution. As much as I don't want to say it, some people are asking to get fired - and if that's the case, and if there's truly nothing to can do to bring them around, then you need to let them go. That's part of good leadership, too.

You're not going to be able to please everybody - it's impossible to. I mean seriously, it's impossible for six people to agree on what movie to go watch on a Saturday night, much less come to mutually satisfactory terms about everything that needs to be done for your business. But the more you engage others in the decision-making process, the more connected and important you make them feel, the more successful your enterprise is going to be.

Unless your business is politics. Then all bets are off.

A Word About Managing the Millennials

Since I know that managing young workers is a favorite topic on the speaking circuit these days, I'd like to weigh in. In 2009 I wrote a book called "How to Get Fired!: The New Employee's Guide to Perpetual Unemployment", which was designed to help high school and college students successfully transition into the working world by telling them everything they shouldn't do once they get hired. I still speak at high schools and colleges around the country, because amazingly enough, not everybody alive has gotten around to reading my book. I don't know what everyone's problem is.

Anyway, I imagine that you've had some trouble with some of your younger employees. It's possible that you think most of them are lazy, disinterested, unmotivated, and entitled – that is the stereotype of Generation Y, and in many cases it is a dead-on accurate one. I'm guessing you've read a few books about how to manage young workers, or that at the very least you've listened to speakers talk about the various techniques you can use to reach this new, techno-savvy, ADHD generation of "workers".

And I'm guessing that everything you've heard has annoyed you. Because you don't want to change. And you definitely don't want to cater to them. After all, *you* are employing *them*, so why should you have to be the one to make concessions to their model? Why should you have to change the way you operate just to accommodate a bunch of spoiled kids that whine about everything and expect to get promoted every two weeks despite their complete lack of work ethic?

So before we even talk about how to manage them them, I want to talk about *why* they are the way they are. There are two fundamental differences between older generations and people 25 and younger. This information might be true of some of your older employees as well, and so it might also help you manage your older employees better – but I can absolutely guarantee that it's true of everybody who fits into the "Generation Y" label.

The first thing that I want you to understand is this:

Despite all outward appearances
and all evidence to the contrary,
the members of Generation Y
are the *loneliest* generation
that has ever lived in this country.

It's the absolute truth. And the reason for that is because of how the world has changed in the last twenty years.

If you're over 25, then you grew up in a world without constant connections, just like I did. I remember writing letters by hand and waiting a couple weeks to hear back from my pen pals. I remember that mile-long phone cord in the kitchen that allowed you to talk in two or three rooms of your house – oh, sweet mobility! I remember cell phones that came with their very own purse, just like those field telephones they used back in World War II. And I remember spending four hours putting a mix tape together that would probably only ever be heard by a single other person on Earth. Because *that's* how you showed a girl that you liked her.

What's the point I'm trying to make? It's that you and I developed our sense of self in a relatively small community, the way we're designed to. Whether you ascribe to a religious or secular view of the where people come from, you have to admit that for the overwhelming majority of human history, we have defined ourselves through small groups of people. In your case, you had your neighborhood, elementary school, high school, or college – a few hundred people, possibly a few thousand. And in a world that size it's relatively easy to carve out a position for yourself, something that grounds you, something that assures you that you're being noticed. You might not have liked the position that you found yourself in, but you knew you had one.

For kids today, though, who have *always* had the Internet and *always* had 500 channels of television, their world has *always* been global. They did not develop their sense of self in the same bubble we did; they've tried to discover who they are in a crowd of six billion others. And in a world that large, it is significantly harder to feel like you're being noticed by the world at large. That's a large part of the reason that in the last two decades everybody started putting their diaries online. Call it a 'blog' all you want, people - it's a diary.[4] The diary used to be an opportunity for personal reflection, something you didn't share with anybody - now, though, it's a way to get attention, to try and force the world to notice and value you, which young people are absolutely desperate for.

It's the same reason that young people tend to have hundreds of friends on Facebook and followers on Twitter. Let's be honest - nobody has 1,000 friends. I have thousands of acquaintances and hundreds of relationships, but I probably have around 50 people outside of my family that I would consider friends, and I talk regularly to fewer than 10 of them. But they have hundreds and thousands of them, or *appear* to at least. The collection of connections on social media is another way that young people attempt to make the world pay attention to them. Unfortunately for them, though, social media provides the illusion of society; it is a poor replacement for the kinds of connections you find only in the physical company of others. In a strange way, social media often acts to keep people separated from one another (I'd go into more detail on that, but it'd be a book in itself). And all of that means that the more connections young people make online, the harder it is for them to explain why they feel lonely considering how many 'friends' they seem to be surrounded by.

Please understand, this phenomenon is not limited to young people. Technology has changed the way that all of us interact. It's made the world impossibly large for every one of

[4] Personally I don't like the word 'blog' because it sounds to me like you threw up a little. "Are you OK?" "No, I just blogged, I need to lie down."

us, and so it is difficult for every one of us to feel that what we do on a daily basis is important, valuable, or worthy of attention, especially when every day you can see the best-parts version of somebody else's life on YouTube and any number of television channels. But again, you and I grew up in a world small enough to allow us to develop that sense of self that protects us a little from the negative effects of all this technology. Today's young people never got that protection. And so all they know is that they've been dropped into an impossibly large world where everybody is shouting always about everything. And what they want more than anything is for somebody to come along, pluck them out of this endless ocean of noise, and make them feel like they're not drowning.

And what's worse, they'll never be able to articulate that loneliness to you, because they don't know there's another way to think. This hyperconnected world is the only one they've ever known. So they'll probably never think to tell you how they feel, or how desperately they crave real recognition. You'll just have to know it.

That's the first difference. The second is this – I am 32 as I write this sentence, and I am saying this with absolute confidence:

Everybody my age and younger has been told our entire lives that the world is *not* going to take care of us.

For the last twenty years, young Americans have been bombarded with that unfortunate idea. There will be no pensions; there will be no Social Security; there will be fewer and less comprehensive health benefits; we are going to be the first generation that lives less well than our parents; and the second our employers can figure out how to automate our job or outsource it somewhere cheaper, they're going to do exactly that.

Now I know that's not how it is everywhere. That might not be how it is at your company. But that's what we've been told – that is the prevailing ethic of our time. Fifty years ago, the idea was that loyalty was repaid with loyalty; people worked their entire lives for a single company, and that company provided lifelong security. That wasn't true for everyone, either, but that's the idea that's been passed down to us. Today, the concept of loyalty has been replaced by something much closer to every-man-for-himself.

What does this have to do with young workers? It means that before you even see a resume, the person who sent it to you is already assuming that you don't care about them. Young employees are not coming to you as a blank slate; they're coming with a deficit of trust, a deficit that in many cases has nothing to do with you.

So you've got young employees coming into your workplace who are simultaneously desperate to belong to something and who have been trained to believe that you're not going to care about them. Which is why a lot of them show up to work with no intention of caring about their job – unfortunately, they don't see the point. They've watched all the outsourcing, they've seen the reduction in benefits, they've paid attention to the steady transition many companies have made from full-time employees to 1099 or LTE arrangements, and they do not want to invest themselves in something only to be disappointed.

I don't expect you to like this. It's frustrating for both parties. But if you want to keep young employees around for a while, then you need to let them know as early as possible and as often as possible that you care about their well-being – not just the work they do, but who they are as people. If you don't want them to use you as a placeholder until they find a better job, you need to let them know that you're not using them as a placeholder until you find a better or cheaper alternative.

And you know what? You don't have to make any grand gestures. In most cases, you don't even have to spend an extra dollar. There are any number of small things you can do to make young employees feel like you care about them:

- Give them business cards and personalized nameplates on their first day of work
- Learn their names *immediately*, and make a point of walking past their desk to say hello on a regular basis
- Invite them to lunch once a week, or at least once a month
- As with your other employees, ask them what they want out of their job over and above salary and benefits
- Give them an early opportunity to take a leadership role in a small project
- Tell them on a regular basis the things that they're doing well (this will also give you an easier opportunity to tell them the various things they need to work on improving)

In short, do anything and everything you can think of to make them feel like you notice and appreciate them.

Please note: *you cannot create a work ethic in somebody who does not have one;* that is a separate issue, and unfortunately you will probably have to suffer through a few young employees who expect the world to be handed to them without doing anything to earn it.

But you *can* create an environment where young workers see the benefit of working. You *can* create an environment where they can look at you and your company and think that maybe yours is a place worth working for. And it doesn't take much more on your part than to change a little about the ways you communicate.

A Word About Change Management

Uh-oh. I said the word 'change,' didn't I? RUN FOR THE HILLS!!!

But I'm already committed, so let's talk about change. Here I am, telling you to forge open and honest lines of communication with everyone you work with, to deal with a new generation of workers, to occasionally have difficult conversations with disaffected employees – and all that might sound like something different than what you've always done. And we all know how much people hate to do things differently, right? After all, that's what all the books about change management say.

And there are a *ton* of books about change management. I'm sure you've read a few. I have. And even though you didn't ask for it, let me tell you what I think of all of them:

Every book ever written about change is terrible.

I hate all of them. They are an affront against human dignity[5], and it is my hope that Congress eventually passes a law that bans their publication.

Why do I dislike them so much? Because they all say the same thing. Every book I've ever read that focuses on change management makes the same central argument, and it goes something like this:

Change is coming and inevitable – so instead of fighting against it, you should learn how to accept it and incorporate it into your working model.

Every one of these books - EVERY ONE OF THEM - presents the issue of managing change as though it is a new skill, something you have no understanding of, and something that you will need to work on.

And that is one of the dumbest arguments I've ever heard people in the world of business make - and believe me, that's saying something. Because in case you haven't noticed, change is absolutely the natural order of things. You are not the same person that you were a year ago, or five, or twenty, and you will not be the same person in one or five or twenty years. Our country is nothing at all like it was when we colonized it. Our Founding Fathers never argued about

[5] Especially the ones that attempt to teach through allegory. "Hi, stupid reader! I know you'll never understand what I say if I simply talk like an adult, so let me share my ideas through the charming story of a couple of mice!"

climate change, or gay rights, or health care. In fact, health care in colonial America was the same for every American, and you know what it was? Whiskey. Strong whiskey and a stout stick. Our health care plan 250 years ago was as follows:

Health Care, Colonial Style!

1) Drink this.
2) Bite on that.
3) We're going to operate.

And everything else you can think of has undergone a similar, inexorable transformation. I may never meet you, but I'm still perfectly comfortable saying that your business is not the same as it was two years ago. You're working on different projects now than you were a few years ago, with different people - and even if by some miracle you're doing the exact same work with the exact same people as you were two years ago, you're doing it in different ways. You're using different equipment, dealing with new regulations, mastering new technologies, navigating new or evolved relationships with your business partners. Nothing stays static. That's possibly the only real truth of the natural world.

Still don't believe me? OK, then. Let me show you some of my favorite examples of change. A while back I stumbled upon a training manual that a Fortune 100 company used back in 1956. This training manual is not actually for employees, but for the *wives* of employees. I'm pretty sure that there isn't a company in America that still publishes a manual designed to help women behave like good company wives anymore, but let's let that go for a moment. Read these over and tell me if anything in them looks like anything you had to read when you got hired wherever you currently work:

Actual Printed Sentences in a Training Manual for a Fortune 100 Company, Circa 1956

- "Give him the pleasant picture of the girl he took for his life's companion by grooming yourself to be attractive and neat."
- "Even if your husband likes to rise and eat alone, set the table the night before and leave the kitchen and living room in an orderly state, so he will leave home with a renewed impression of your good housekeeping."
- "Try to harmonize with his mood, but especially before he leaves for work. If he likes companionship before he leaves for work, give it to him."

That last one, by the way, is the most amazing pair of sentences I have ever read in my life. Because I can't remember the last time I got 'companionship' before I left for work – and now my company is ordering it! That's awesome! "I don't even want this, sweetheart, it's for the company!"

I can't believe any of those sentences were ever able to be written, but I am dead certain that you couldn't write any of those now; you'd be sued in about 8,000 different ways. But this was the way of things back in the 1950s. Today, however, things are a little bit different.

The point I'm trying to make here is that change happens continually in every element of life, both personally and professionally. And you know what? Most of the time *you don't even notice*, because it's so natural. The only time any of us worries about change is when somebody tells us it's happening - and then, for some inexplicable reason, we all freak out. And there's no reason to.

You know how I know that you're probably perfectly OK with change, even though I've never met you? Because I'm going to guess that you are either a parent, or someday plan to become one. Most people are or will be. I am not a parent yet, by the way. And every so often I make the mistake of telling people who have children that I would someday like to become a member of the parenting club.

And in case you're a parent, I would like you to know something: you absolutely, positively, undeniably suck at selling the idea of parenthood. Have you ever listened to what you say to people like me? You're *awful!*

Example of Conversation I Always Have with Parents About Parenthood

Me: "I think I'd like to be a parent someday."

Parent: "Well. Hope you don't like money. Or privacy. And you might just want to get all of your sex out of the way now, because you're not going to have any once those kids come around. I'm really excited for you, it's the best decision you'll ever make."

To hear you tell it, parenthood is an endless war of sleeplessness, worry, and self-sacrifice. Couple that with the scenes every non-parent has seen of screaming children in supermarkets and shopping centers across the country, and there seems to be precious little to recommend the idea of parenthood.

But you know the other thing that parents say, every single one of them? That it's *different* when it's *yours*. That something happens when your children are born that you could not understand until that moment. You had no idea what you were getting into. You thought you did; you'd seen other parents, you'd discussed what it would be like, you'd agreed upon the techniques you would use and the mistakes you would avoid. But raising your children does not follow any plan that you had in place. They come along, and you spend the rest of your life running to catch up. The decision to become a parent changes us more profoundly than probably any other decision we will ever make. And I know a lot of parents occasionally lament their single days and their childless days, when they could do whatever they wanted whenever they wanted without having to answer to anybody. But I also know that if you are a parent, you probably wouldn't go back if you could. I know that what your children have given you so far outweighs what they've taken that it isn't really even a consideration anymore.

I hope that example makes some sense – but even if it doesn't, here's my point. You've incorporated thousands of changes into the person you are today. You've done it continuously, seamlessly, effortlessly, and in most cases without even noticing that those changes are happening. And because of that, you should not fear the changes that are coming in your professional life any more than you've ever feared the changes you've dealt with very easily throughout your personal life. The art of managing change, whatever that change is, is nothing new or foreign. You've been doing it your entire life. If there is one skill that everyone in the world is an expert at, it is dealing with and managing change. And the reason all of us are experts is that, when it really comes down to it, we've been given no choice.

I won't pretend to know what changes you're facing in your professional future. I'm sure there are several. Maybe you have a new boss, or new employees; maybe you're rolling out a new product or dealing with a new method of communicating with your clients; maybe you're being assigned an international role or being asked to learn a new process; maybe you're opening a new facility or merging two divisions into a single unit. I'm sure you're excited about some of these changes and nervous about others. But I can tell you this: whatever changes you're about to face, they will require no new skills on your part. I'm not saying you have to like everything that's coming, but I can guarantee you that you have nothing to fear. And I hope that knowing that will allow you to face the changes that are coming to you with a little more equanimity than you might have otherwise.

A Word About Taking Responsibility

We're almost done. I know you're anxious to get to whatever Facebook game or reality show you're currently addicted to. Don't worry – your time is coming.

But we still have to talk about responsibility. As I'm sure you're nauseatingly aware of, the mark of true leaders is taking responsibility for their actions, the good and especially the bad ones, because it's impossible to learn from your mistakes until you admit that you've made them. You've probably heard that a million times, and by now it's such a cliché that it doesn't hold a lot of transformative power anymore.

So let's look very briefly at *why* most of us are so quick to blame others for our mistakes. I think knowing the causes for our behaviors are a good way to find a cure for them. And here's what I think causes this practice:

At our core, I believe all of us are terrified that the world is someday going to realize that we are a complete fraud.

I think all of us believe that, to a certain extent, we're just making it up as we go. We have no real idea what we're doing, we've been faking it our entire lives, and we worry that someday the world is going to figure that out and expose us for the charlatans that we are. I don't think it's a paralyzing fear in most of us, but I think it exists in just about everyone. It certainly does in me.

And I think that fear leads to two outcomes. First, it contributes to our resistance to change. After all, nobody's figured out that you're a fraud yet, right, so let's just keep things the way they are so that they never will. But we've already addressed everyone's natural expertise at adapting to change, so while this is an understandable concern, it isn't exactly a valid one.

The second consequence, of course, is that we are usually very quick to look for scapegoats for our mistakes and failures. We blame others in part so that we can continue to fool people into thinking that we're better than we believe ourselves to be.

There's just one problem with it. It doesn't actually work.

Oh, it works in the short-term. Sometimes the practice of blaming others works for years. But odds are, given a long enough timeframe, people will eventually discover that you've never taken responsibility for anything. In that way, one's sense of personal responsibility functions a lot like a Ponzi scheme. If you're ever caught lying or blaming others for your own problems, people will very quickly stop trusting you – and once that trust is broken, it can be impossible to ever get it back.

Look back at some of the most famous corporate debacles of the past 25 years – Enron, WorldCom, Adelphia. Do you know what destroyed those companies? It's not the creative accounting – lots of companies do that, and it doesn't always lead to that company's complete destruction. And it's not that they had a bad product or too much supply and not enough demand. Fundamentally, what destroyed all of them was their loss of reputation. People had absolutely no faith left in anything those companies said, and it crushed them.

And the same forces that govern a company's reputation work on an individual level as well. A person's reputation is inextricably linked to how they handle themselves. People who are caught lying, or blaming others for their failures, often find their reputations ruined overnight. As Warren Buffett says, "It takes 20 years to build a reputation and 5 minutes to ruin it."

How is that possible? Because reputation is a remarkably fragile thing. One poorly-handled situation can undo years of otherwise responsible behavior. People tend to form their opinions of others based on a tiny amount of information. Throughout this book I've given you very little information about any of the people I've held up as tyrants – sometimes four things, sometimes as few as one – and usually that's enough for us to begin to form a solid opinion of who we think a person really is.

I'll prove it. Earlier in the book I talked about John Henry Patterson, the founder of National Cash Register and a man that you had probably never heard of until now. I talked about his habit of capriciously firing employees, his antitrust activities, and his penchant for choking people. It would seem that his character is quite firmly established.

So let me tell you a little more about John Henry Patterson.

Profiles in Tyranny?
John Henry Patterson

Best known to readers of this book as a man who liked to choke women, John Henry Patterson was one of the first people in the American Industrial Revolution to insist upon humane treatment of his employees. After seeing a picture of one of his female workers warming her coffee over a radiator, he offered a complete hot lunch to all female employees. A dining room for 400 women was built in 1895. The result? The percentage of his employees missing work due to illness (often caused by poor nutrition) dropped from 18 percent to 2 percent in one week.

Patterson opened the first 'daylight factory' anywhere in 1893, so called for the floor-to- ceiling windows that could be opened to let in fresh air, as well as light. Other industrialists accused him of being too easy on his workers, and many were appalled when he installed ventilation hoods, locker rooms, women-only restrooms, in-plant healthcare, gymnasiums, and landscaped grounds that employees could enjoy during their breaks.

His generosity didn't stop there, either. In 1913 a massive flood overwhelmed the town of Dayton, Ohio. In response, Patterson gave food and shelter to displaced Ohioans, as well as supplying electricity and fresh water. When the United States entered World War I, Patterson's factories were outfitted for the production of timers and airplane instruments, which he insisted were produced on a 'fixed fee' rather than 'cost plus' basis. He is said to have been "proud not to have made any money on the country's necessity."

When Patterson died in 1922, he left behind very little money, due largely to his investment in social programs, company welfare initiatives, and the war effort. With respect to his modest fortune, Patterson died exactly as he wanted to. In his own words: "Shrouds have no pockets."

That doesn't exactly paint the picture of a cruel and malicious man, does it?

Here's another example. Do you remember the quote I shared earlier from Theodore Roosevelt? Here it is again:

"The best executive is one who has sense enough to pick good people to do what he wants done, and self-restraint enough to keep from meddling with them while they do it."

It's an excellent summation of good leadership. But what if instead of *that* quote, I'd used *this* one, which Roosevelt also said?

"I don't go so far as to think that the only good Indians are dead Indians, but I believe nine out of ten are, and I shouldn't like to inquire too closely into the case of the tenth."

That changes your perception a bit, I'm guessing. And if that were the *only* thing you knew about Roosevelt, it would probably give you a much different vision of who he was.

The point is this. Every person has a multitude of qualities, some good and others not so much. Almost nothing in this world is black and white. And yet, we tend to form our opinions of others very quickly, with very little information, and those opinions tend to stay with us for a long time. It does not take much for people to start passing judgment. And it is an unfortunate truth of humanity that we tend to focus on problems - and the resolution of those problems - more than anything else. That's the basis of modern news and entertainment: there is a problem somewhere, so let's see how that problem gets taken care of.

Which means that whenever a problem comes along, it has a greater potential for ruining your reputation than anything else. You undoubtedly know that. But it is the *handling* of that problem that will determine how people view you. There's all kinds of evidence to support the idea that customers who have experienced a problem with a company that worked quickly and honestly to resolve the issue are *more loyal* than customers who have experienced no problems at all.

The early admission of a mistake actually causes people to think more favorably of you than if you never made the mistake in the first place. Because we *expect* things to run smoothly, but we are *impressed* by people who correct things when they don't.

One of the most famous corporate examples is the 1982 Tylenol cyanide crisis. Someone injected cyanide into several Tylenol capsules at stores throughout Chicago, leading to the deaths of seven people. It was not Johnson & Johnson's fault - they were very quickly found to be not responsible for the contamination - but the company nevertheless went on an immediate offensive, recalling every bottle of Tylenol in production at an estimated cost of $100 million.

The damage in the short-term was considerable: Tylenol's market share plummeted from 35% to 8% in just a few months. But the long-term benefits were even more striking. The media applauded Johnson & Johnson's swift and honest approach in dealing with the issue. Sales of Tylenol rebounded within a year. And more importantly, Johnson & Johnson cemented itself in the public mind as a trustworthy and responsible company.

Flash forward to a modern example of taking (or completely avoiding) responsibility: Tiger Woods, and David Letterman. Both men were guilty of having affairs, and both stories became public at approximately the same time. The big difference between them - aside from quantity, of course - is the way they handled their particular crises. Tiger Woods attempted to dodge the issue, to avoid and delay as long as possible. David Letterman, on the other hand, actually broke the story before anybody else had a chance to. He admitted guilt in the most public way possible, and by doing so he owned and controlled the conversation. As every good comedian knows, if you make fun of yourself first, nobody else really can. Neither man was admirable in the way they behaved, but they chose to handle their mistakes in very different ways.

The end result? David Letterman's reputation is intact. Advertisers did not abandon his show; ratings remained stable; and a decent number of people have probably forgotten that the incident even happened. For Tiger Woods, however, his attempt to avoid responsibility backfired in a massive way. He lost his marriage, millions of dollars in endorsement deals, his reputation as a role model for children - and unless things change, he seems also to have lost his position as the best golfer in the world. At this printing, he's fallen out of the world's top ten.

The earlier you accept responsibility for problems, the faster they go away. It is not a foolproof plan - sometimes the problems that come are too severe to be handled. Certain problems really are the end of the road. I hardly think that John Edwards would have been able to save his political career by freely admitting his affair before others discovered it. Obviously, the best approach to good leadership is to never make any mistakes at all. But when you do make mistakes, addressing them early and taking responsibility for them is the *only* way that you might be able to prevent problems from spinning out of control.

Oh, and did I mention that blaming others for your mistakes is one of the quickest ways to make people hate you? Or that it's probably the most effective way to lose the respect of your employees? I feel like I said that somewhere, didn't I? I can't remember…

The Last Words I'm Gonna Say

So here it is, my aspiring leader. I hope you've enjoyed, had a few laughs, but I'd like to leave you with the honest takeaways, if for no other reason than to convince you that there actually are some. So here they are:

The Point of This Whole Stupid Book!

- **Your org chart is a measure of position, not importance.** Everybody in your organization is important - and at the very least, everybody believes that they are important. Remember that, and treat people like they matter, and you'll be repaid several times over.

- **Get to know your employees as *people*, not just as *employees*.** Another way to put this is 'Avoid treating your employees as disease-infested bags of stupid,' but I thought that first one sounded a little more professional. This is important for you to do with all your employees, but doubly so for your younger ones. If you want to keep them, that is.

- **Burn all of your self-appraisals.** They tell you nothing. N-o-t-h-i-n-g. And they allow you to maintain a separation between yourself and your employees that is not healthy for either of you. I know it'll take a little more time to have an actual conversation with each of the people who work for you, and I'm sorry if the prospect terrifies you. Deal with it.

- **Trust the people who work for you.** Your employees manage to feed and dress themselves every day; it's possible that they are capable of handling other tasks as well. Besides, if you truly can't trust them, they should not work for you.

- **Listen to everyone, and let them know that you're listening.** This is my nice way of saying, "Every so often, shut the hell up." If the story of General Electric and the Work-Outs didn't convince you, nothing will.

- **Accept the fact that mistakes are an inevitable and necessary part of becoming better.** You weren't always perfect yourself, and don't pretend otherwise. I know you've made a handful of terrible decisions in your life, and if I could look at your music library I could prove it quite easily. I've got some songs on my iPod that should never have been written. But more importantly, every success is built on a foundation of multiple failures. All of them.

- **Tell people what they need to hear when they need to hear it.** Even if – especially if – it's difficult. That's the key to being a good husband, wife, son, daughter, or parent, and it's the key to being a good leader as well.

- **Remember that the rules which govern your personal relationships are the same rules that should govern your professional relationships.** Fundamentally, all human interactions operate within the same set of laws and rules. So the things you do at work shouldn't be too much different from the things you do at home.
- **Beware the compliment sandwich.** Gottman's 5:1 hypothesis, and the studies he conducted to reinforce his argument, are very compelling.
- **Remember that change is natural, and that you are already an expert at it.** 'Change' is also the reason you are hopefully less annoying now than you were when you were four. You don't have to like every change that comes your way, but you certainly have no need to fear any of them.
- **Take your share of the blame, and give away your share of the credit.** The credit you give away will return to you, usually with interest.
- **Give people an opportunity to do what they do best.** And if you don't know what they do best, then talk to them and figure it out.
- **When possible, avoid engaging in massive accounting fraud.**

I've actually taken the liberty of printing these concepts on a single page at the end of this chapter. They are the major points in every leadership book that's ever been written. Tear it out, put it in your wallet, and you should never have to read another leadership book for the rest of your life. If we are ever lucky enough to meet, you can thank me for saving you hours and hours of your life by buying me a drink, or perhaps a go-kart. I've always wanted one of those.

Leadership is not a difficult skill to master. It takes little more than the ability to talk to others. It requires you not to believe that you know more than you do, or that your employees know less than they do. It forces you to remember that your every action is communication of one kind or another. And it means you need to do the opposite of just about everything I've said - except for this chapter, of course.

So there you have it. You now have the tools to be whatever kind of leader you wish to be - benevolent or tyrannical, beloved or despised. You can be the kind of person that people commission a statue for, or you can be the kind of person who commissions a statue of yourself that others will eventually topple over and melt down as soon as you're gone.

The choice is yours.

Summary of Every Leadership Book Ever Written – Past, Present, and Future

Your org chart is a measure
of position, not importance.

Get to know your employees as people,
not just as employees.

Burn all of your self-appraisals.

Trust the people who work for you.

Listen to everyone, and
let them know that you're listening.

Accept the fact that mistakes are an inevitable
and necessary part of becoming better.

Tell people what they need to hear
when they need to hear it.

Remember that the rules which govern
your personal relationships are the same rules
that should govern your professional relationships.

Beware the compliment sandwich.

Remember that change is natural,
and that you are already an expert at it.

Take your share of the blame,
and give away your share of the credit.

Give people an opportunity to do what they do best.

When possible, avoid engaging
in massive accounting fraud.

Sources

Finally. After all the waiting, you're finally to the section you were waiting for. This is easily the most riveting, captivating, enthralling section of the entire book. I wouldn't be surprised if you neglect your children for the next few hours as you drown in the magic of these next few pages.

You're welcome. Enjoy.

Jeff Havens

P.S. I probably forgot to list a few sources here, but I'm not overly worried about it. And why am I so calm and collected about it? Because I'm pretty confident that nobody is actually going to read past this sentence.

Preface:

Trust: The One Thing That Makes or Breaks a Leader. Les T. Csorba. Oliver Nelson, 2004.

First, Break All The Rules: What the World's Greatest Managers Do Differently. Marcus Buckingham & Curt Coffman. Simon & Schuster, 1999.

Establish Positional Dominance:

http://en.wikipedia.org/wiki/Harry_Cohn

http://gawker.com/5383421/larry-ellison-struts-his-wealth-before-peons

http://www.management-issues.com/2007/9/11/blog/some-bad-boss-statistics.asp

http://en.wikipedia.org/wiki/Dennis_Kozlowski

Create Grandiloquent Titles For Yourself:

http://en.wikipedia.org/wiki/List_of_titles_and_honours_of_Queen_Elizabeth_II

http://www.wellingtone.co.uk/blog/?p=104

http://en.wikipedia.org/wiki/Joseph_Stalin

Remain Aloof and Above:

www.crea.coop/.../SELLING%20SAFETY%20TO%20**EMPLOYEES**.doc

Thinking Inside the Box: The 12 Timeless Rules for Managing a Successful Business, Kirk Cheyfitz, Free Press, 2003.

Tough Management: The 7 Ways to Make Tough Decisions Easier, Deliver the Numbers, and Grow Business in Good Times and Bad. Chuck Martin. McGraw-Hill, 2005

Managing for the Short Term. Chuck Martin. Currency/Doubleday, 2002.

The End of Management and the Rise of Organizational Democracy. Kenneth Cloke & Joan Goldsmith. Jossey-Bass, 2002.

The Management Century: A Critical Review of 20th Century Thought and Practice. Stuart Crainer. Booz Allen & Hamilton, 2000

How Full Is Your Bucket? Positive Strategies for Work and Life. Tom Rath and Donald O. Clifton, Ph.D. Gallup Press, 2004.

http://www.businessweek.com/magazine/content/04_44/b3906112.htm

http://www.referenceforbusiness.com/biography/F-L/Kelleher-Herb-1931.html

First, Break All The Rules: What the World's Greatest Managers Do Differently. Marcus Buckingham & Curt Coffman. Simon & Schuster, 1999.

http://www.management-issues.com/2007/9/11/blog/some-bad-boss-statistics.asp

Bureaucracy...

http://thinkexist.com/quotations/bureaucracy/

http://www.ttgconsultants.com/articles/trustworkforce.html

Tough Management: The 7 Ways to Make Tough Decisions Easier, Deliver the Numbers, and Grow Business in Good Times and Bad. Chuck Martin. McGraw-Hill, 2005

The End of Management and the Rise of Organizational Democracy. Kenneth Cloke & Joan Goldsmith. Jossey-Bass, 2002.

The Management Century: A Critical Review of 20th Century Thought and Practice. Stuart Crainer. Booz Allen & Hamilton, 2000

http://en.wikipedia.org/wiki/UBS

"Swiss bank UBS to change much-mocked dress code" FRANK JORDANS, Associated Press, Monday Jan 17, 2011

Trust No One:

http://ezinearticles.com/?The-Importance-of-Trust-in-the-Work-Place&id=552339

http://www.cult-branding.com/article/please-trust-me.html

http://badergroup.com/the-value-of-building-trust-in-the-workplace/

Business the Rupert Murdoch Way: 10 Secrets of the World's Greatest Deal-Maker. Stuart Crainer. American Management Association. 1999.

Micromanagement!

http://ww.management-issues.com/2009/10/16/opinion/keeping-up-in-a-down-economy.asp?section=opinion&id=5755&is_authenticated=0&reference=&specifier=&mode=print

Winning Behavior: What the Smartest, Most Successful Companies Do Differently. Terry R. Bacon & David G. Pugh. Amacom, 2003.

Thinking Inside the Box: The 12 Timeless Rules for Managing a Successful Business, Kirk Cheyfitz, Free Press, 2003.

The 360 Degree Leader: Developing Your Influence from Anywhere in the Organization. John C. Maxwell. Nelson Business, 2005.

http://www.nytimes.com/1997/11/23/business/harold-s-geneen-87-dies-nurtured-itt.html

Talk more Than You Listen:

How Full Is Your Bucket? Positive Strategies for Work and Life. Tom Rath and Donald O. Clifton, Ph.D. Gallup Press, 2004.

Managing for the Short Term. Chuck Martin. Currency/Doubleday, 2002.

The Management Century: A Critical Review of 20th Century Thought and Practice. Stuart Crainer. Booz Allen & Hamilton, 2000

http://news.bbc.co.uk/2/hi/7745324.stm

Sucking Like a Champion: Overcommunicating

http://gogreengiants.com/the-art-of-over-communication

Demand the Impossible!

http://www.brainyquote.com/quotes/keywords/impossible_7.html

Tough Management: The 7 Ways to Make Tough Decisions Easier, Deliver the Numbers, and Grow Business in Good Times and Bad. Chuck Martin. McGraw-Hill, 2005

First, Break All The Rules: What the World's Greatest Managers Do Differently. Marcus Buckingham & Curt Coffman. Simon & Schuster, 1999.

http://en.wikipedia.org/wiki/Outliers_%28book%29

Create Double Standards!

The End of Management and the Rise of Organizational Democracy. Kenneth Cloke & Joan Goldsmith. Jossey-Bass, 2002.

http://en.wikipedia.org/wiki/Angelo_Mozilo

Focus on the Negatives!

Partnering: The New Face of Leadership. Larraine Segil, Marshall Goldsmith & James Belasco, editors. American Management Association, 2003.

How Full Is Your Bucket? Positive Strategies for Work and Life. Tom Rath and Donald O. Clifton, Ph.D. Gallup Press, 2004.

Why Marriages Succeed or Fail. John Gottman. University of Washington, 1995.

Threaten Physical Violence!

Working with Difficult People 2nd edition. William LUndin, Ph.D, Kathleen Lundin, Michael S. Dobson. American Management Association, 2009

http://www.slate.com/id/2063218/

http://sportsillustrated.cnn.com/vault/article/magazine/MAG1095174/index.htm

http://sportsillustrated.cnn.com/2004/basketball/ncaa/02/03/knight.timeline/

http://en.wikipedia.org/wiki/John_Henry_Patterson_%28NCR_owner%29

Create Win/Lose Situations

http://www.adeccousa.com/articles/What-Makes-a-%22Best-Boss%22.html?id=168&url=/pressroom/pressreleases/pages/forms/allitems.aspx&templateurl=/AboutUs/pressroom/Pages/Press-release.aspx

http://www.digitalhistory.uh.edu/database/article_display.cfm?HHID=203

http://en.wikipedia.org/wiki/Jay_Gould

Hoard Credit:

How Full Is Your Bucket? Positive Strategies for Work and Life. Tom Rath and Donald O. Clifton, Ph.D. Gallup Press, 2004.

Trust: The One Thing That Makes or Breaks a Leader. Les T. Csorba. Oliver Nelson, 2004.

Sucking Like a Champion – Charging People...

http://www.foxnews.com/story/0,2933,501780,00.html

http://blogs.villagevoice.com/dailymusto/2010/04/airline_might_c.php

When in Doubt...Lie!

Tough Management: The 7 Ways to Make Tough Decisions Easier, Deliver the Numbers, and Grow Business in Good Times and Bad. Chuck Martin. McGraw-Hill, 2005

http://zfacts.com/p/581.html

http://ezinearticles.com/?Disconnected-and-Disengaged?-Reconnect-Your-Employees-to-Exceptional-Performance&id=1283967

Avoid Risk!

http://www.highbeam.com/doc/1G1-123792046.html

Think Short Term:

Business the Rupert Murdoch Way: 10 Secrets of the World's Greatest Deal-Maker. Stuart Crainer. American Management Association. 1999.

Managing for the Short Term. Chuck Martin. Currency/Doubleday, 2002.

Create an Escape Plan for You and Nobody Else!

The Power of WE: Succeeding Through Partnerships Jonathan M. Tisch, Chairman & CEO, Loews Hotels. With Karl Weber. John Wiley & Sons, Inc. 2004

Managing for the Short Term. Chuck Martin. Currency/Doubleday, 2002.

http://en.wikipedia.org/wiki/Richard_S._Fuld,_Jr.

http://en.wikipedia.org/wiki/Stan_O%27Neal

http://en.wikipedia.org/wiki/Martin_J._Sullivan

When All Else Fails...Company Sabotage!

http://en.wikipedia.org/wiki/Stuart_Parnell

The Truth About Leadership

The Management Century: A Critical Review of 20th Century Thought and Practice. Stuart Crainer. Booz Allen & Hamilton, 2000

The 360 Degree Leader: Developing Your Influence from Anywhere in the Organization. John C. Maxwell. Nelson Business, 2005.

Influencer: The Power to Change Anything. Kerry Patterson, Joseph Grenny, David Maxfield, Ron McMillan, Al Switzler. McGraw-Hill, 2008.

http://home.paonline.com/knippd/whoisncr/Patterson.htm